Talk Turkey to Me

a good time in the kitchen
talking turkey and all the trimmings

Renee S. Ferguson

Wishbone Press and Promotions | Illinois

ISBN: 0-9777321-3-4
Library of Congress Control Number: 2006921154

Published by Wishbone Press and Promotions Inc.
      PO Box 414, Glen Ellyn, Illinois 60137
      info@talkturkeytome.com | www.talkturkeytome.com

Photographs: Renee Ferguson
Digital photo retouching: Steve Sellers
Illustrations: Mary Austin and Martin Austin

10 9 8 7 6 5 4 3 2 1

Printed in Canada.

All product/brand names are trademarks or registered trademarks of their respective trademark holders.

Disclaimer: We have taken care to ensure that the information in this book is accurate. However, we can give no absolute guarantees as to the accuracy or completeness of the content of this book. We accept no liability for any losses or damages (whether direct, indirect, special, consequential, or otherwise) arising out of errors or omissions contained in this book.

Produced by Callawind Custom Cookbooks
A division of Callawind Publications Inc.
3551 St. Charles Boulevard, Suite 179, Kirkland, Quebec H9H 3C4
2059 Hempstead Turnpike, PMB 355, East Meadow, New York 11554-1711
E-mail: info@callawind.com   Website: www.callawind.com
Copy editing and indexing: Jane Broderick | Design: Marcy Claman

acknowledgments

Many generous family members, friends, and acquaintances helped me in a variety of ways to bring this book to fruition. Special thanks go to my husband, Johann, and my children, Erin, Dallas, and Kyle, for believing in me and for being the best cheerleaders any writer could ever want.

I offer warm thanks to those outstanding women who shared their time-honored recipes, graciously allowed their heirlooms to be used in photographs, and encouraged me through countless conversations; to Judy Olson and Deb Skarnulis for being selfless, loyal, and giving friends who make me laugh out loud; and to the scores of contributing food consultants and set designers: Nardine Alsobrook, Martha Bouchard, Bonnie Butters, Karen Crab, Anis Duncan, Lisa Easley, Doris Ferguson, Nancy Gouch, Ann Grabski, Camille Grabski, Mary Heath, Laura Hintz, Sherry Hirsch, Ingrid Kerr, Judy Kinn, Judy Lammering, Cathee Laughlin, Sara Lee, Maria Martinez, Kyle McDougal, Melody Merrick, Lucy Newman, Sarah Peck, Ruth Loving Ramon, Alice Redpath, Kathy Sayers, Kathy Snodell, Terry Spahn, Cheryl Swift, Maggie Triplett, and Carleen Urban.

I am grateful to Steve Sellers for his unique abilities with digital photography. His patience and guidance are greatly appreciated.

The artistic and creative talents of both Mary and Martin Austin are acknowledged and greatly appreciated.

I would like to thank the many anonymous men and women who have kindly and good-naturedly shared their predicaments with me, enabling me to put pen to paper and write this book. Special thanks are due to Butterball® for helping people to celebrate Thanksgiving for more than half a century. I am particularly grateful to the women of the Butterball® Turkey Talk-Line® for their many years of professionalism, generosity, and personal kindness.

Thanks as well to Judy Martin, owner of The Perfect Thing, for allowing me to come into her antique store and photograph sets using the beautiful antiques there.

Many thanks to Spike Odell, who was an unwitting source of encouragement and quiet tenacity, allowing me to stay the course and move forward with my idea.

Every book needs an editor and I enthusiastically thank Jane Broderick for her talents and for keeping me focused. A special thanks to Marcy Claman for being a sounding board, artist, teacher, and production coordinator in guiding this book on its journey to publication. You are the greatest!

table of contents

Talk Turkey to Me is a spirited and playful how-to book that will guide you humorously as you prepare a perfect turkey for any occasion. It features an assortment of cooking methods. Whether you choose to prepare your turkey the traditional way—roasted in the oven—or on a grill or rotisserie, roasted upside down, or even cooked from frozen (yes!), you'll find that this cookbook is like no other. The pages that follow contain detailed instructions for more than 20 cooking methods and how to achieve a picture-perfect turkey every time. Our "call girl," Renee Ferguson, provides straightforward answers to questions from the call-in turkey hotline, an essential resource for those legions of people who find themselves with a case of "turkey trauma" when it comes time to prepare their holiday meal.

This comprehensive, step-by-step guide will help you to plan a special feast or an everyday dinner by recounting amusing questions and comments by hotline callers. The helpful but lighthearted responses of our hotline "call girl" make for lively and entertaining reading.

Turkey is the ultimate comfort food. A turkey dinner usually conjures up images of traditional holiday meals with family and friends. Now you can have that feeling year round. Turkey is making an appearance on menus throughout the year, whether it's at a backyard barbeque, Fourth of July celebration, everyday dinner, or any of a multitude of holiday gatherings. Low in carbohydrates, fats, sodium, and cholesterol, turkey is a popular choice among the food-conscious, from South Beach, Atkins, and Sugar Buster dieters to those who are simply concerned with healthy eating. Yet for all of its nutritional benefits, turkey still manages to maintain a comfort-food profile.

A turkey dinner offers the versatility of that little black dress in every woman's wardrobe. It's the subtle backdrop to the accessories of your outfit—or to the side dishes of your meal. The main course that isn't prepared properly, like the little black dress that doesn't fit properly, can ruin your entire evening.

Callers' kitchen trials and tribulations are recounted by our hotline "call girl." Ferguson uses each amusing question or anecdote to guide the reader through the various steps and methods of turkey preparation. Many of the questions will have you chuckling. Just as with reality television, the reader becomes a voyeur, listening in on the everyday cooking challenges faced by so many people. Used as a reference, the book offers quick and easy answers—but don't be surprised if you find yourself caught up in the questions and answers as you thumb through the pages.

Most cookbooks approach the cooking task from a basic, one-size-fits-all perspective. They assume you'll be cooking your turkey either in an oven or on a grill and simply give you the required cooking times. Well, one size does not fit all. Maybe you intend to roast your turkey in an oven bag or in Grandma's covered roaster. Or perhaps you forgot to thaw the bird! Dovetailed with the variety of methods described in these pages are questions and stories from callers that will help to enlighten you in an entertaining way.

Beyond turkey triumphs and challenges, the book includes a collection of tried-and-true recipes for starters, side dishes, desserts, and various accompaniments. Experienced cooks as well as novices who have never so much as picked up a cookbook before will enjoy trying out these recipes. They may even discover a dish or three that will become part of their holiday celebrations for years to come.

So whether you have a convection oven and can't find the instructions, or are trying to master a water smoker for the first time (or the twentieth), in this book you'll quickly find your answer, your funny bone, and how to prepare your turkey perfectly, from grocery bag to table.

let's begin to talk turkey

Does Size Really Matter?

"Let's see, there'll be four big men, two little girls, and five women. They're Asian and I'm from Iowa. So how much turkey will I need to buy? I don't want to run short. I'd be so embarrassed."

The first question on everyone's mind is how much to buy. The greatest fear of every host is running out of food. There's an easy rule of thumb for estimating what size turkey you'll need to purchase. If you like to have leftovers, plan on 1½ pounds per person. This takes into account the weight of the bones, juices (or "drip weight"), giblets, and packaging. But if you're having the football team over maybe you'd better plan on more per person!

"My husband bought the turkey and it's so big it looks like it's nesting on top of

the roasting pan. I'll get a bigger pan, but what was he thinking? There are only two of us. We'll just have to call some college students over to help us eat it. They can eat you out of house and home, but even then we'll have enough!"

If you want to have enough for a great day with ample portions but little or no leftovers, plan on 1 pound per person.

The caller briefly recounted his work history and told me he was a sous-chef. He explained that the sous-chef is the person who ranks next, after the head chef, in a restaurant kitchen. It seems that a dispute had arisen between the head chef and the sous-chef. The caller didn't want to upstage the chef but did want to have the matter settled.

"How should we estimate how much turkey to purchase if we want to have leftovers? I already know the answer, but I just want to hear it from you and settle our disagreement."

BUYING GUIDE*	
Number of people	Size of turkey (pounds)
8	12
10	15
12	18
15	22
18	27

*Based on the recommended 1½ pounds per person, allowing for leftovers.

"Can you tell me how much my turkey weighs?"

This is not a psychic hotline and I am not Miss Cleo, but if the turkey label is missing and you don't know how much your turkey weighs, simply put it on a bathroom scale and weigh it.

Fresh versus Frozen

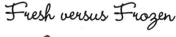
"How do I thaw a fresh turkey?"

A fresh turkey is just that—fresh, not frozen. As it requires no thawing time, it's ready to cook. One of the hazards of buying a fresh turkey is the tendency to ignore any dates that may appear on the label. Consider when your dinner is going to be and plan accordingly, buying your fresh tur-

key no more than a few days ahead. Although many advances have been made in packaging and refrigeration, everything has a limited life span: once the wrapper has been cut or compromised, the clock is ticking toward spoilage. Always cook the turkey within 3 days of the "sell by" date.

I love the questions that start with "What would you do?"

"What would you do? The expiration date on my turkey was 4 weeks ago. It's been held in the refrigerator the whole time . . . is it okay?"

Well, what would you do? Food begins to spoil even in your refrigerator when held beyond the recommended time.

"Are there taste differences between fresh and frozen?"

Most definitely. Though the differences may be subtle, each type has its own taste. I recommend that you try both fresh and frozen to find out which you prefer.

How fresh is fresh? The commotion was evident. Clearly, the woman was calling from a cell phone. I could hear the kids in the background and the panic in her voice.

"We live on a farm in the country. We raise our own turkeys every year and I have four of them in my truck. You know, turkeys stress out real easily—chickens don't; they're cool. We're on our way to slaughter and I think one of them is having a heart attack. The kids are really upset and they're trying to calm him down. I tried playing soothing music, but this is one really stressed turkey and I think he'll be a goner before I'm ready. I still have a long way to drive. How long do I have before it's too late to use him?"

*W*hole fresh turkeys have a limited shelf life. Frozen turkeys have the convenience of extended life. The downside is that they take time to thaw. Many a person has called in a panic, stating that they didn't know the turkey had to be thawed before cooking.

Frustration abounded in this caller's voice:

"My family is not gonna want to deal with this menopausal woman. My fresh turkey is partially frozen. Help me!"

*T*urkeys freeze at a much lower temperature than water, and it may be that your turkey has ice crystals in the cavity. Run cold water through the turkey; this should resolve the problem.

Thawing: A Complete Guide

An Alabama woman called about what she described as a "freezer museum." She was phoning on behalf of her father-in-law. He had been a widower for only a short time when he decided to tackle the job of cleaning out the freezer. Apparently his dear departed wife was the type who never threw things out.

Among the cryogenically preserved antiquities were:

- snowballs in a Ziploc® bag labeled from a long-past snowstorm
- the top tier of their wedding cake
- a turkey in the original wrapper with a tag indicating that it was from 1969

"Is this turkey safe?"

There's good and bad news here. The good news is that it's safe provided it has remained frozen the entire time it has been maintained in its suspended state. The bad news is that while it may be a safe turkey it will not be a tasty one, as extended freezing removes the moisture from food no matter how well it is wrapped or stored. And when moisture is removed from meat, a dry and tasteless product is left behind. This is one turkey I would not recommend eating.

National Thaw Your Turkey Day

The Thursday before Thanksgiving is National Thaw Your Turkey Day. No matter how big or how small your turkey, it's time to take it out of the freezer and put it in the refrigerator. Small turkeys that thaw in 3 to 4 days still can be safely held in the refrigerator if kept in the original wrapper and at a refrigerator temperature of 40°F or lower.

"I've got a flock of 'bingo' turkeys in my freezer. I'm just lucky—I win every time I go. I've got one turkey that's been there longer than a year. I'm not sure we shouldn't have a birthday party or a coming-out party when I go to thaw him. Since he's been in the freezer longer than the others, will he take longer to thaw?"

No matter how long your turkey has been in the freezer, it will take no longer to thaw than the times listed in the guide at the right.

"I don't know how much my turkey weighs. It's been in the freezer and the tag is gone. How long do I thaw it?"

There's no complex mathematical formula for estimating the time required to thaw a turkey. However, you'll need to weigh the bird on a bathroom scale in order to determine how many days it will need to thaw in the refrigerator (according to the guide at the right).

"My neighbor told me to split the wrapper when the turkey is thawing in the refrigerator so the gases can escape and I won't have a rotten bird."

Sounds as though Miss Information kept her turkey thawing way beyond the recommended time! If gases were forming, it was already starting to spoil.

Follow the convenient guide below to thaw your turkey safely in the refrigerator. (The day you place it in the refrigerator doesn't count. For example, if you plan to cook your turkey on Sunday and it has to thaw for 2 to 3 days, start thawing it on Wednesday or Thursday.) Be sure to place a tray underneath the turkey to collect any juices that seep through the wrapping.

REFRIGERATOR THAWING GUIDE	
Net weight (pounds)	Thawing time (days)
7 to 10	2 to 3
10 to 18	3 to 4
18 to 22	4 to 5
22 to 24	5 to 6
24 to 30	6 to 7

Quick-Thaw McDraw Cold Water

"I need to thaw a turkey fast for church and don't want to make anyone sick. I'd hate to have to beg for their forgiveness after they got well!"

Stay on the straight and narrow path by using the quick-thaw method to thaw your turkey safely . . . no confessions needed!

"I've never been a successful turkey person and I have to thaw my turkey in the bathtub. The turkey is floating in my tub now. I have a scuba belt that I could harness onto it to hold it down under water if that would help."

Here's a quick-thaw method. Partially fill the sink with cold water. Place the turkey breast-side-down in the water so that it's like an iceberg, with the largest part submerged. The turkey itself will float, so don't worry—it need not be fully submerged. The U.S. Department of Agriculture recommends that you change the water every 30 minutes. The thawing time is easy to calculate: just divide the weight by two, and that's the number of hours needed to thaw the turkey in cold water.

"Talking to you is like talking to my therapist. I know I'll feel better afterward—and, better still, you won't send me a bill! But I still feel insecure about knowing if my turkey is thawed."

"I'm not sure if I'm going to make the list of Top 10 Boo-Boos, but my turkey is not entirely thawed. It's been in the refrigerator for 4 days and it's still not thawed."

If, when you remove the wrapper, you find that the turkey has not thawed completely, you could run cold water through the cavity to melt any ice crystals that may have formed, or you could just begin to cook the turkey. If you do begin to cook it, the turkey should not be stuffed, and it will take longer to cook than usual. Either way, when cooking the turkey be sure to use a meat thermometer in order to determine when the correct end temperature is reached.

COLD-WATER QUICK-THAW GUIDE

- Leave the wrapper on the turkey.
- Divide the weight by two to determine the number of hours needed to thaw it in cold water.
- Change the water every 30 minutes.
- Place the turkey breast-side-down in the water. The turkey will float!
- Sanitize the sink when finished.

A young man called to ask, *"Can I thaw this thing in an electric blanket?"*

The day before Thanksgiving, a wonderful middle-aged woman called and emphatically stated, *"I know how to cook and you're not dealing with an idiot, but I have an 18-pound turkey—when do I start to thaw it?"*

Running short on time? Electric blankets are not recommended. It's best to thaw your turkey in cold water . . . even if you're not an idiot!

Timing Guide for Cold-Water Quick-Thaw Method	
Net weight (pounds)	Hours
8	4
10	5
12	6
14	7
16	8
18	9
20	10
22	11
24	12

Other factors that can affect thawing time

- glass shelves in the refrigerator: these restrict the flow of air, which is needed to thaw the turkey
- the temperature setting of your refrigerator
- the amount of use the refrigerator gets: if you have a house full of kids constantly opening and closing the refrigerator door, the rate of thawing will be sped up; conversely, if the turkey is placed in an extra fridge that you rarely use, there will be no warm air admitted from outside and thawing will take longer

"My grocer said it would only take 3 days to thaw this 20-pound turkey. Is that right?"

Check the thawing guide on page 12. Whom are you going to trust, someone who's thawed scores of turkeys or a person who's probably never cooked a turkey in his life? A solid block of frozen meat takes a long time to thaw. Give yourself extra time to make certain the process is complete.

Some common-sense rules

- Do not thaw at room temperature, as this will cause bacterial growth to increase on the surface of the turkey before the inside is fully thawed.
- Allow ample time for the turkey to thaw in the refrigerator; use the thawing guide on page 12.

Urban legend?

Scientists at NASA have developed a gun built specifically to launch dead turkeys at the windshields of airliners, military jets, and the space shuttle, all traveling at maximum velocity. The idea is to simulate the frequent incidence of collisions with airborne fowl to test the strength of the windshields.

British engineers heard about the gun and were eager to test it on the windshields of their new high-speed trains. Arrangements were made. When the gun was fired, however, the engineers stood in shock as the turkey hurtled out of the barrel, crashed into the shatterproof shield, smashing it to smithereens, crashed through the control console, snapped the engineer's backrest in two, and became embedded in the back wall of the cab.

The horrified Britons sent NASA the disastrous results of the experiment, along with the design of the windshield, and begged the American scientists for suggestions.

NASA's response was just one sentence: "Thaw the bird."

Source: Numerous Web sites.

- Keep the turkey in its original wrapper to prevent drying of the skin and to reduce the risk of cross-contamination.
- It makes no sense to thaw a turkey in the microwave (even though this method of thawing is approved by the U.S. Department of Agriculture). The configuration of a turkey, with large, thick areas and smaller, thin areas, leads to uneven thawing. Parts of the bird will begin to cook before other parts are thawed. This is not the best option.
- Once the turkey is thawed, use it within 4 days.

One week before the big day, a procrastinator tried to mend the error of her ways only to run into trouble.

"I'm a procrastinator, but this year I sat up all night and thawed the turkey in cold water and changed it every 30 minutes. Now I'm afraid it's thawed too soon. Do I have to cook it now, or can I keep it refrigerated until the party? If I have to cook it now, it'll be like a James Bond movie and we'll have Turkey Galore!"

Once your turkey is thawed you should use it within 4 days. Again, be sure to keep it in the original wrapper. If you've already removed the wrapper, cover the turkey with plastic wrap or with foil, or seal it in a food-safe storage bag, and store it in the refrigerator. Remember, being thawed is being completely thawed. It's like being pregnant . . . either you are or you aren't.

Preparing the Turkey

"I'm a first-timer," the caller declared. "Forty-one years old and I've never done this before. This sucker is so big. When do I take it out to thaw?"

"Not to worry," I said breezily. "Just place the turkey breast-side-up on a tray and put it in the refrigerator."

"Which is the breast? The big bump? I always get mixed up. Even at Colonel Sanders I get the breast and the thighs mixed up—I mean on chickens, not women. Hey, I'm a guy! But when the leg portion gets cut off, that's when I get confused."

Everyone has a first time. But regardless of how you plan to cook your turkey, there are steps to follow. These are:

- Remove the wrapping from the turkey.
- Drain the turkey over the sink and check both of its cavities. One holds the neck and the other the bag of giblets. Remove these and either reserve them for use in your recipes or discard them. Some people like to cook them

for either themselves or their pet—it's up to you!
- Blot the exterior of the turkey dry with paper towels.
- Stuff the turkey if desired.
- Bend the wings behind the back of the turkey (optional). This is a sexy little move meant to hold the neck skin in place, but it's not really necessary.
- Brush or spritz the turkey with oil, and season if desired.
- Insert an oven-safe meat thermometer into the turkey.

"We just realized we cooked the turkey with that bag of stuff still inside of it. Do we have to throw the whole turkey out?"

No—it's okay. But don't use the neck or giblets, as they may not have cooked to the proper end temperature and could pose a food-safety risk.

One consumer called with a note of fear in her voice. She was afraid someone had tampered with her turkey. It seems that when she unwrapped it she found a large hole between the legs and a smaller hole between the wings. She wondered if the holes should be there or if the turkey on her counter was a victim of product tampering.

All dressed and ready for a hot date in the oven!

$\mathcal{R}$est assured that the holes in the ends of the turkey are supposed to be there. The larger hole is the body cavity and the smaller one is the neck cavity. This is where the stuffing is to be placed, if you choose to stuff the turkey. During preparation, be sure to check both ends for the giblets and neck and remove both packages.

"I'm newly married and we're pregnant and I feel like I live on Stupid Street. I've never done this before and I know I have to wash the turkey. My husband said that it's just like washing a baby and to just hold it under a shower of water—and that I should get used to it . . . the baby will be here before we know it!"

$\mathcal{G}$ood news. You don't live on Stupid Street and you don't have to practice Baby Bathing 101 on the turkey. There's no need to wash or rinse a turkey, chicken, fish, or any meat product you plan to cook. The cooking process will kill any bacteria that are present. That's the purpose of cooking—not to mention the fact that it enhances the taste! But truly, the reason we don't wash turkeys, or any other meat products, is to minimize the splashing of raw juices. Scattered drops of raw juices can inadvertently splash other food products and cross-contaminate them.

Prepping the turkey and roasting it are easy to do despite attempts by many to complicate the matter. Simply place the turkey on a rack in a shallow, open pan. If you're using a disposable roasting pan, place the pan on a baking sheet for support. Most disposable foil pans have some "bumps" on the bottom that act as a rack, helping to keep the turkey out of its juices as it cooks.

Brush the skin with oil, or use a cooking spray to add moisture to the skin.

WHY OIL?

"Should I wipe the turkey dry or massage oil into it?"

Everyone could use a massage before the party. Go for it!

Vegetable oil results in more even browning than butter, which tends to produce tiny brown specks on the skin. However, some people are passionate about their choice of "massage oil." Choose whatever makes you feel better!

A sweet-voiced elderly woman described her method of moisturizing the turkey's skin before putting it in the oven:

"I pamper my turkey. I take two sticks of butter and, in a circular motion, I rub it all over the turkey—just like a facial rub!"

This simple and easy method of preparation will become second nature to you. Just remember to follow the steps:

- Place the turkey in the sink. Remove and discard the wrapper.
- Drain the juices from the turkey into the sink.
- Pat the turkey dry with paper towels. Discard the paper towels.
- Place the turkey on a rack in a shallow, open pan.
- Rub the turkey with vegetable oil for even browning, or simply spray with a cooking spray—it's a lot less messy and there's no brush to clean.
- Season the turkey if you wish.
- Insert an oven-safe meat thermometer into the turkey.

Seasoning: The Spice of Life

"I lived in Barbados for a while. Those people rub everything with ketchup. How do you think it would be if I rubbed my turkey with ketchup?"

"Our family uses maple syrup to baste the turkey. It's sweet and crispy and it browns the turkey nicely."

"My mother is from the Old Country. She's always done this and I've been cooking

since I was 13 so I do it too. Everyone just loves my turkey in tomato sauce!"

"I just watched this cooking show and they used pickling spice to season the turkey. What do you think of that?"

Seasoning is a matter of personal preference. In reality, any seasoning that is sprinkled or rubbed on the turkey will not flavor or penetrate the skin or the ribs. The skin is a barrier—it keeps substances from getting into the meat. Think about your own skin. If you sprinkled oregano on yourself, it wouldn't seep through your skin and flavor your insides! The only part of the turkey that gets flavored is the skin itself—as well as the pan drippings.

Trends in seasoning change, just as recipe ideas featured in magazines change from year to year. Whatever choice of flavors is your passion, just remember to follow the timing guide for the specific cooking method you will be using. The only thing you really need to do is keep it simple.

"Do I season this all over the turkey body and make it look more ugly?"

"My buddy puts garlic under the skin, but I don't want to put my hand in there!"

"What about apples, oranges, and an onion in the cavity or sprinkled around the outside?"

"I use mayonnaise instead of oil."

Some people use a dry rub, while others marinate the turkey using their favorite seasonings. The variations are countless. There may be as many recipes as there are cooks, and they can range from simple to complex. Some people feel that if they don't shake something onto the turkey they are just aren't cooking it at all!

Permission granted. If you want to season the turkey with salt and pepper before roasting, go ahead, but know that any seasoning that you sprinkle on top of the bird or place in the cavity will not affect the flavor of the turkey and may affect the flavor of the gravy. Your only essential ingredient is oil. Everything else is superfluous.

"I put this herb paste that has rosemary, thyme, and sage under the skin of my turkey. It's all green now and looks like it's ready for St. Patrick's Day. I can't put a green bird in the oven without my husband running to the deli and ordering out! Who comes up with these recipes?"

Anatomy 101

> "Thank God you're there! I've been divorced for 14 years and never cooked a turkey. Tell me, what's this little wing part? I didn't know turkeys had wings."

"I need some confirmation. I thought when I got a whole turkey it would be all white meat. There's dark meat on this one."

Approximately 70 percent of a whole turkey is white meat. The remaining 30 percent is dark meat. If you want only white meat, purchase a breast.

> "My mother-in-law did everything. She spoon-fed all of us, including me, and after 10 years she's no longer around. Which is the neck end and where do I put the stuffing? She'd be aghast that I couldn't figure out what this big hole is!"

"I bought a turkey and the directions said to put it breast-side-up. Where's the breast and which side is up?"

The breast is the big bump that faces up when the turkey is placed flat on its back. If you were to place the turkey breast-side-down, it would be a rock'n and roll'n bird.

"My husband is in the navy. He says a hen's breast is bigger than a tom's. Does a hen have a bigger breast?"

It's not like human anatomy. Your husband's been in the navy too long!

"That hook, the bony, butt part—do I take it off?"

Not if you belong to this family:

"That part that goes over the fence last is the piece of the turkey the men in our family all fight over. Each year we have to draw straws to see who gets the honor of eating it. It started when I was a kid and each year we'd argue about it because Dad always got it since he was the dad. Now that he's gone, my brothers and I figured out a fair way to win the pièce de résistance."

That pièce de résistance, by the way, is the turkey's tail.

Giblets

> "I didn't get that bag with the—you know—personal parts."

In one cavity of the turkey when you purchase it is a bag containing the heart, liver, and gizzard. This trio is what are called the giblets. In the other cavity you'll find the neck. All or part of the giblets and neck may be used to make a broth and then stored for use in any of your favorite recipes that call for broth.

> "I'm newly married and I understand how to cook the turkey and everything, but what I don't get are these giblet things. What is this stuff? I don't want to ask my husband because I don't want him to know that I don't know these parts."

"You mean I have to put my hand in there? Look, I'm straight . . . I just don't want to run into anything I shouldn't!"

The giblets are the heart, liver, and gizzard of the turkey. The heart is triangular in shape and reddish brown in color. The liver is flatter and is also reddish brown, with a slippery feel. The gizzard has a bluish coloration.

To some people, this ménage à trois is a staple of life that, once cooked, finds its way into recipes for stuffing, gravy, or soup. To others, it's a nuisance bag that gets thrown away or fed to the cat. This is an emotional topic for those who view the giblets as the key to a successful holiday feast.

"The jury's still out and trouble's brewing! How many bags are in the turkey?"

You should find two, one in the neck cavity and one in the body cavity. That's all!

TRADITIONAL GIBLET BROTH
Simmer the neck, heart, and gizzard in 3 cups of salted water for 2 hours. Add the liver and simmer for another 20 to 30 minutes. For extra flavor, you may add the following to the neck, heart, and gizzard: 1 small onion (chopped), 1 stalk of celery (chopped), 1 bay leaf, and ½ teaspoon of dried thyme. When the cooking is complete, strain the stock and discard the vegetables.

The cooked meat may be chopped and used in stuffing, gravy, or particular recipes. The broth may also be used as a liquid in stuffing, soup, or wherever needed.

"I just took Mr. Turkey out of the refrigerator and there aren't any goblets—I mean giblets—in him."

Don't get your giblets in a knot if your turkey is without them. Even purists find that in a pinch a broth made from chicken parts—legs, thighs, and wings—will substitute for the missing goblets—er, I mean giblets!

Is it a he or a she?

The world is made up of tom turkeys and hens—along with those cross-dressers that are labeled simply "turkey." Generally, a tom weighs in at 16 pounds or more. Toms are male turkeys. A hen typically weighs less than 16 pounds. Hens are female turkeys.

One caller was surprised that, year after year, no matter what the weight of the turkey, she always wound up getting a male. When I asked her how she knew this, she replied, "Well, I always look inside and pull out that little bag of personal parts, and, sure enough, every year it's a tom!" Apparently the caller mistook the neck for another part of the male anatomy . . . I can only visualize that turkey strutting around the barnyard!

"I have the weight of the world on me today. My day is ruined. There are no giblets inside the turkey!"

Courier companies don't realize the fortune they could make with a giblet exchange on Thanksgiving Day. Those who simply toss out the bag of personal parts could be united with those who feel as the above caller did. Although to some the giblets are worth their weight in gold, don't let the absence of the little bag spoil your feast. Just fake it and try substituting the giblets with a broth made from chicken parts. Count your blessings and move on.

Stuffing

You know there's a problem when the caller opens the conversation by saying, "Poison Control gave me your number."

To stuff or not to stuff, that is the question. There are as many opinions about stuffing safety as there are recipes, but here's the bottom line: if the stuffing has been prepared properly, placed in the turkey just before roasting, and cooked to a temperature of 160°F, it's perfectly safe. Here are a few tips for proper food handling when it comes to stuffing:

- Do not prepare your stuffing in advance.
- Do not stuff your turkey the night before.
- Do not use uncooked meats in your stuffing.
- Do not use eggs in your stuffing (an egg substitute is acceptable).
- You may sauté your vegetables and meat in advance, but do not toss them with the broth and the bread cubes or crumbs until you are ready to stuff your turkey.

Talk Turkey to Me

- When taking the final temperature of the turkey, also take the temperature of the stuffing. The thermometer should read 160°F when placed in the center of the stuffing.

"Now that I've made my stuffing, can you tell me if I put it in the front door or the back door?"

How about both? Loosely stuff the neck cavity and cover with the large flap of skin that you see. Hold the floppy neck skin in place with the wing tips that have been bent back behind the turkey. Lightly stuff the main cavity and don't worry about the portion of stuffing that protrudes from the opening; it will cook and form a crust.

RECYCLING QUEEN I
"Is it okay if I use an old nylon for a stuffing bag?"

Nylons and panty hose are not food-safe items. The World War II effort to recycle nylon didn't include cooking with it. Not a good idea!

A Philadelphia lawyer had just one question: *"Do I stuff it from the beginning or cook it halfway through and then stuff it?"*

Always stuff your turkey just before cooking it.

Stuffing recipes are highly prized. Many are family treasures, as evidenced in a call from a fun guy (you could tell by his voice . . .):

"After 22 years of marriage we divorced and I didn't get her mother's stuffing recipe. I forgot to have it entered as part of the divorce decree. I've asked other family members whom I'm friendly with to give me the family recipe but I don't have it yet."

After some reflection, he remembered . . . *"Oh, my ex called and she's going out of town . . . I think I'll call my ex-mother-in-law! I get along great with her—she can't understand why her daughter divorced me. I'll give her a few glasses of wine and she'll give me the recipe."*

The Truth about Basting

Basting is really therapy for the cook. It makes you feel as though you're doing something to help your turkey reach a deep golden-brown color. In reality, though, basting doesn't help the browning process at all. Your turkey will brown all by itself. Furthermore, basting does not penetrate the skin, so any effort to "flavor" the meat or keep it moist will be wasted. In fact, because you're opening and closing your oven door so often, the oven will cool down and hence your turkey will take longer to cook. Why do you think it took Grandma all day to cook her turkey? She was in and out of the oven a zillion times!

"Are all of your turkeys self-basting? It doesn't say on the label?"

Any turkey or chicken will turn a wonderful golden brown without your help. Just brush the skin with oil and roast uncovered for the first two-thirds of the cooking time, then tent the breast for the final one-third.

After the first 15 minutes in the oven, the turkey's skin becomes seared, so pouring juices on it is like pouring water on a plastic tablecloth—the liquid will simply roll off.

"Oh, you have such smart turkeys!" said the caller when I told her there was no need to baste her turkey—the bird would do everything all on its own.

"Yes, we educate them in the basics before we send them to market," I replied.

The caller continued with her anxious questioning, asking whether she should rinse the turkey in water. When I told her there was no need for this, she thought for a moment and then said, *"Hmmm—smart, educated, and practices good hygiene. Too bad I can't find a man like that!"*

Determining Doneness

After being told to check the temperature of the thigh, the caller dutifully did so, and then announced that her thighs needed to get hotter!

"I won't eat at my grandchildren's house. They don't use a meat thermometer!"

Compelling testimony from a grandma! A meat thermometer completely eliminates the guesswork in cooking turkey, or any other meat or poultry. It must be important if it would keep a grandma from dining with her grandchildren. A thermometer costs little, and once you've used one you'll wonder how you ever cooked without it.

"I just pulled my meat thermometer from the drawer and it reads 140ºF. I'm toast! How do you know when the turkey is done if you don't have a thermometer?"

If you just don't have a meat thermometer, the old-fashioned method of piercing the lower thigh with a fork to see if the juices are running clear will have to do. The color of the skin is not an indication of doneness. Even if the skin is brown, it may be that the outside just cooked too quickly because of a high oven temperature. Conversely, the skin could be pale simply because you used a covered pan and the turkey itself could be done. Poke around with a fork to pierce the lower parts and check to make sure the juices are running clear.

One caller, apparently confused, set her oven temperature at 160°F. Confusion abounds among chefs and home cooks alike when it comes to oven temperatures and final cooking temperatures. If you were to cook your turkey to an end temperature of 160°F, the meat—though safe to eat—would be very rare and have an unappetizing quality and texture; the juices would be very pink and the meat would be chewy. So, for optimum taste and visual appeal, it is recommended that the thigh temperature be 180°F.

"I've been in France for five years and engaged to a great guy for about a year. He's a honey but he mentioned the other day that he wanted me to cook a turkey. I told him I'd make a ham but he said he really wanted turkey for the holiday. He thinks I've done it before but I never have and now I'm in a panic. I'm in deep x#@#! I don't have directions. I don't have a meat thermometer. Oh, wait, I'll ask him where his meat thermometer is and he'll just assume I know what I'm doing!"

You'll possess confidence once you have a meat thermometer.

Eliminate the guesswork and just follow these simple guidelines:

COOKING TO THE PROPER END TEMPERATURE
Regardless of the cooking method—whether roasting or grilling—the end temperatures are the same:

- Stuffing 160°F
- Breast 170°F
- Thigh 180°F

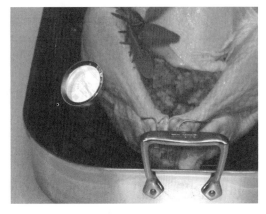

Insert the meat thermometer into the thigh. To determine the right position, push the tip of the thermometer in until you reach the bone, but then pull back slightly so that it does not not actually touch the bone.

"We didn't thaw the turkey. If I cook it from frozen, do I use a drill to put a hole in for the meat thermometer?"

Wait until about halfway through cooking and then insert the meat thermometer, when the meat is soft. (More on this cooking technique later.)

The pop-up timer is actually a funky thermometer. It works simply. The pop-up is constructed using an inner blob of metal that melts at around 185°F. The metal is in solid form at room temperature but will become molten as the flesh surrounding it heats up. When the metal becomes liquid, the pop-up indicator pops as a result of a spring mechanism within the outer casing—and the turkey is done.

A Word about Pop-up Timers

"I've been watching and waiting and it looks done, but this little plastic thing hasn't changed color."

Ma'am, it's not like a pregnancy test—it won't change color.

Your turkey may or may not come with a pop-up timer. This little bit of technology is designed to take the guesswork out of determining when your turkey is done. It may be convenient if you don't have a meat thermometer but should not be the sole indicator of doneness. Check to make sure the juices in the lower parts of the turkey—the leg and thigh—run clear.

"Well, the pop-up timer never did go off, so I continued to cook it for 9 hours. Everyone told me it was delicious and couldn't compliment me enough!"

This turkey roasted for more than triple the amount of time required. The cook was blessed with a patient, gracious, and diplomatic family who were so hungry they would eat anything and think it was good! Common sense should be used with respect to timers that fail to pop. A tradiional meat thermometer is a good backup to a pop-up timer and can also take the temperature of the lower thigh area, which is shielded by the roasting pan. The thigh must reach a temperature of 180°F.

let's talk turkey and the ways to cook it

"I was in college, sharing my first apartment with four other engineering students. Everyone else had gone home for the holiday and we decided to make the best of it by buying a turkey and making it ourselves. Collectively we knew how to boil water but were a little short on the details of how to cook a turkey. How hard could it be? We were engineering students! We bought our turkey and got it home and thawed it. The big day came and we were prepared to make a meal fit for the hot shots we were. We preheated the oven, took the turkey out of the wrapper—and then realized we didn't have a pan to roast it in. The stores were all closed and we frantically went to the neighbors to borrow a pan but no one was home. We went to our landlord but he didn't have one either. He, however, did have a newly purchased galvanized garbage can with a lid, and our engineering minds went wild! Necessity being the mother of invention, we snagged the lid, lined it with foil, and put the turkey on it and into the oven. A few hours later . . . voilà . . . We cooked our turkey rather unconventionally, but it was the product of great engineering minds."

Having the right tools on hand can make a cook's life easier. As resourceful as these guys were, knowing what method you are going to use and cooking the bird according to that method will assure you of a turkey worthy of a Kodak® moment. However, the time required to cook a turkey can vary widely. There are adjustments to be made for each cooking method and for the equipment you'll be using. If you know how to use the equipment properly, you'll have the confidence necessary to prepare a mouth-watering meal.

The following pages tell you how to cook a perfect turkey using any one of more than 20 methods. The simplest way is the open-pan method, as evidenced by the aforementioned creative engineering students. Whether you're using a disposable pan or heavy-duty cookware, this technique will give you consistent results.

Another common way to cook turkey is the covered-pan method. Do not attempt to use the bottom of this unit for the open-pan technique, as you will not get satisfactory results. If you choose to use a covered pan, you must use both pieces of the unit to get the best results.

The majority of methods require the use of an open roasting pan. Other methods, however, involve the use of a convection oven, covered roasting pan, oven bag, covered electric roaster, grill, water smoker, deep-fryer, rotisserie, crock pot, or microwave oven.

No matter which method you select, if you follow the cooking instructions you'll produce the turkey of your dreams.

traditional methods

Open-Pan Method: Effortless Roasting for Chefs and Novices Alike

"I'm from Colombia and newly married. Being South American, I have never celebrated Thanksgiving so this is my first, and I haven't really cooked much before getting married. Yesterday my in-laws dropped off a turkey, dressing mix, and sweet potatoes and expect me to make a full-course dinner. When they left they even told me what time they expected dinner to be ready! What do I do now?"

Looking for a foolproof way to get the best results each and every time? Look no further! The open-pan method is the easiest way to roast a turkey. It consistently gets excellent results. If you want both optimum quality and optimum simplicity, this method is for you. It produces a roasted flavor, tender and juicy meat, and a golden-brown color. Whether you're a novice or an expert cook, count on this technique to bring you a sensational turkey that will have your family and guests applauding you at the dinner table.

"What the heck am I going to do with this turkey? I would have been happy with a Swanson's® TV dinner, but the turkeys were on sale and I invited some people over. Now I don't even know where to begin!"

It's as easy as 1-2-3:

- Remove the wrapping, drain the turkey, and blot the exterior dry with paper towels.
- Remove the neck and giblets from the two cavities.
- Place the turkey breast-side-up in a shallow pan 2½ or 3 inches deep.
- Brush or spritz the turkey with oil.
- Insert an oven-safe meat thermometer into the thickest part of the thigh.

- Place the turkey in a 325°F oven.
- Do not baste or open the oven door for the first two-thirds of the cooking time.
- When two-thirds of the cooking time has passed, the turkey will be a light golden brown. Place a tent of light-weight aluminum foil over the breast and continue cooking.
- Continue to roast until the thigh reaches a temperature of 180°F.
- Let the turkey rest for 20 minutes before carving.

"I'm a newly divorced dad and I've never cooked a turkey before. I want this to be special and to make the picture-perfect turkey for my kids. How do I do it?"

By roasting uncovered first, you achieve a beautiful, appetizing brown color. If you were to reverse the process, covering the turkey first and removing the foil after two-thirds of the cooking time, the right color would be harder to achieve. Your turkey could end up being an unappetizing paleface even though the meat thermometer says it's done. Cooking it any longer to achieve an ideal mouth-watering color would dry the meat out. So it's best to start out with the turkey uncovered and then place the foil lightly over the breast to prevent it from overcooking and over-browning.

This caller was not a candidate for Mensa: *"If I cook it for 3 hours I don't know when it will be two-thirds done. How long is that?"*

OPEN-PAN ROASTING GUIDE		
Weight (pounds)	Unstuffed (hours)	Stuffed (hours)
4½ to 7	2 to 2½	2¼ to 2¾
7 to 10	2½ to 3	2¾ to 3½
10 to 18	3 to 3½	3¾ to 4½
18 to 22	3½ to 4	4½ to 5
22 to 24	4 to 4½	5 to 5½
24 to 30	4½ to 5	5½ to 6¼

ROASTING THE BIG ONE

"It's the size of a baby . . . no, it's the size of a small child! I'm in a little trouble. This turkey is big! My daughter raised it for her 4-H project this year. He's about 40 pounds. I have a really big oven and a pan that he'll fit in, but I don't know how long to cook him."

It's a snap. Just add 30 minutes of roasting time for every 5 pounds over 30 pounds. Therefore, your pet project will need only 1 extra hour in the oven. Just be sure to use a meat thermometer to check all points for doneness.

Secrets Revealed

A college student was prepared to take down all the instructions I could possibly give him. We went through things step-by-step, and as a student he excelled in note-taking. He read the instructions back to me to be sure he understood. When he got to the point where the cook checks the turkey at two-thirds of the way through cooking, he said, "So, I check the turkey at two-thirds time, open the door, put the foil on, and then cook with the door open for the remainder of the time."

Men can only retain so much information when they ask for instructions. Please keep the oven door closed when cooking!

"What's 'trussing'?"

Trussing is something that you don't need to do. Trussing is when the legs are secured in order to make a more compact shape. Today's turkey producers do the job for you, using either a band of skin or a metal or plastic clamp to hold the legs together and tucked under. If by chance this has not been done when you purchase your turkey, you can tie the legs together using kitchen string, or you may choose to simply forego this step. In years gone by, the cavities were stitched closed to hold the stuffing in place. This, too, is unnecessary. Just put the stuffing in loosely, and as the turkey roasts the stuffing that protrudes from the cavity will form a crust. Keep it simple!

"What do you mean, drain the turkey?"

After removing the neck and giblets from the ends of the turkey, simply tip the open end over the sink and let the juices drain. Be sure to sanitize the sink and work area when finished, and pat the turkey dry with paper towels.

"Our turkey has a big plastic clamp hanging on it. Do we leave it on or take it off?"

The leg clamp may be metal or plastic, or a band of skin may be used to keep the legs together and tucked under. Leave it alone.

"I don't have a rack.

If you don't have a rack and aren't using a disposable foil pan, you can improvise by making an aluminum foil wreath. Simply take a large length of foil and scrunch it up, forming a circle. Place it in the bottom of your pan to prevent the turkey from sticking.

"Do I put the oven on bake or broil?"

Bake.

"I've had my oven for over five years and have never used it. How do I preheat?"

Preheating is not necessary.

⊚

"Do I cook it naked or covered?"

Naked for the first two-thirds of your cooking time. Then tent the breast with aluminum foil the size of a half sheet of notebook paper.

"So I take a half sheet of notebook paper and put it over the breast?"

No, use aluminum foil the *size* of a half sheet of notebook paper.

"What do you mean 'tent of aluminum foil'? How big?"

Using lightweight aluminum foil, cut a piece the size of a half sheet of notebook paper. Fold it in the middle and gently place the "tent" over the breast area, making sure not to cover the legs or thighs. Aluminum foil is reflective and will shield the breast from the heat yet allow those legs and thighs to continue to cook, as the legs and thighs need to reach a higher temperature. Roast uncovered first, then foil the breast. As insignificant as it may seem, to reverse the process will affect the cooking time, browning, and end product.

"Shiny or dull side out?"

It doesn't matter.

⊚

Sometimes men hear only what they want to hear . . .

"Okay, so I cook it naked."

Yes, for the first two-thirds of your cooking time, and then shield the breast.

"Feel the breast?"

No, shield the breast.

⊚

"What's 'freezer burn'?"

Freezer burn is a dehydrated, whitish area that results from moisture being pulled from food in the freezer. It is still safe to eat but will not taste good, so the freezer-burned area should be removed.

⊚

"It said to cook it for 3 to 3½ hours but it still looked pink so I cooked it a couple of hours longer and it still looks pink. When will it get done?"

Turkey has a natural pink cast to it, unlike chicken, which is very white in color. So don't expect turkey to be white like chicken when cooked—imagine it more like bridesmaid's pink or a white zinfandel. Use a meat thermometer to determine doneness. Color is not an indicator.

"Why can't you just make it easy and give me the number of minutes per pound?"

In actuality, larger turkeys take less time to cook than smaller ones. So much energy is expended in getting the turkey to begin to cook that once it gets going the larger one will cook faster. If you used minutes per pound you'd overcook your turkey, so a range of times are given. Also, the cooking time is different for each method. Check at the earliest time point in the range given; your turkey may be done then.

Convection Oven

| "My old oven would barely heat. Now I have a new convection oven and I don't know how to use it."

The convection oven is debuting in all kinds of new or remodeled kitchens, but many cooks are uncertain about how to use it. Noted for its fast approach to food preparation, the convection oven will significantly reduce the roasting time of your turkey. Because hot air circulates within the oven, the color of the cooked turkey is a reddish, mahogany brown and the skin is wrinkled and leathery-looking, but the taste is superb! The skin has sealed in the juices and you can expect the turkey to have a full, roasted flavor very similar to that of traditional oven-roasted turkey.

"So the turkey will come out different from in a regular oven, just a little more wrinkled and darker brown . . . kinda like Grandma in Florida!"

Preheat the oven to 325°F. Prepare the turkey as usual and, using a shallow, open roasting pan, roast according to the guide below. Do not cover with aluminum foil at any time as the foil will hinder the flow of air circulating within the oven.

"I told my dad I think we're screwed. I think I've ruined the whole thing. I hear sizzling in the pan . . . is that okay?"

For those unfamiliar with the sound of food cooking in their home, this is a natural part of the cooking process. Keep on keeping on!

CONVECTION OVEN ROASTING GUIDE		
Weight (pounds)	Unstuffed (hours)	Stuffed (hours)
6 to 10	1½ to 2	1¾ to 2½
10 to 18	2 to 2½	2½ to 3¼
18 to 22	2½ to 3	3¼ to 3¾
22 to 24	3 to 3½	3 ¾ to 4¼

Covered Roasting Pan

"My mom was a physician in Wisconsin. She was trained in Europe. I'm now 75 years old and I take care of her—she's 102. I think I'm losing it a bit because I should know and I can't remember: do I use the lid the whole time?"

From the speckled roasting pan to the shiny aluminum steel-clad roaster, America's love affair with the covered-pan method has been passed down from generation to generation. No more complicated than the open-pan method, this method produces its own distinct flavor. The turkey cooks within a steamed environment because it is covered, and this makes it cook more quickly. The lid must be removed during the final half hour to let the turkey brown.

"Do I need to add water to the bottom of the pan? And what about rotating the turkey? When my wife was alive she used to rotate the turkey."

It is preferable to not use water or any other liquid at the start of cooking. The drippings will caramelize in the bottom of the pan and become more flavorful without the addition of water. If liquid is used at the beginning, the drippings will be less concentrated and therefore less tasty. It is best to add water or broth to the pan drippings after the turkey has roasted, in order to make a flavorful gravy.

And forget about rotating a huge, hot turkey. Keep it simple and go watch the game!

"Oh, cover—put the lid on! I thought you meant to put the turkey in the lid."

No.

"We went to a charity event where they were bowling with frozen turkeys. My husband brought home the turkey that he used but the directions are lost. How long will it take to roast it in my grandma's speckled roasting pan?"

Covered-Pan Roasting Guide		
Weight (pounds)	Unstuffed (hours)	Stuffed (hours)
4½ to 7	1¾ to 2¼	2 to 2½
7 to 10	2¼ to 2¾	2½ to 3¼
10 to 18	2½ to 3	3¼ to 4
18 to 22	3 to 3½	4 to 4½

Note: A turkey placed in a shiny stainless steel pan may take up to an hour longer to cook. Stainless steel is a poor conductor of heat; it reflects rather than absorbs heat and acts much like a space suit, protecting the turkey from the heat of the oven.

"I plan on rotating the turkey and have invited two other guys over to help me turn the pan."

Not necessary . . . but if you need an excuse to have them share in the preparation of the feast this is as good an excuse as any. Now go back to the game!

Oven Bag

One woman told of her brother-in-law's glory day in the kitchen. He prepared his turkey in an oven bag and set the oven at 500°F. He cooked the turkey for 6 hours and when he opened the bag and stuck a fork in it, the turkey went "poof" and crumbled into pieces—much like the turkey in *Christmas Vacation* with Chevy Chase. The caller had one comment to add about the cook: "He's such a jerk!"

The results of cooking with an oven bag are similar to those using a covered roasting pan. The turkey may or may not brown as perfectly as those featured in the November magazine food layouts. It's very important to remember that color is not an indication of doneness and you must test for doneness at the proper times to avoid overcooking. Again, a meat thermometer is key to determining when the turkey is done.

- Preheat the oven to 350°F.
- Shake 1 tablespoon of flour into a turkey-sized oven bag.
- Place several slices of onion and a chopped celery stalk in the bottom of the bag.
- Brush the turkey with oil; you may or may not stuff it.
- Place the turkey breast-side-up in the oven bag and tie the bag securely. Put it on a rack in a shallow, open roasting pan.
- Make several slits in the top of the bag to let the hot air escape.
- Insert a meat thermometer through the bag and into the thigh.
- Roast until the thermometer reads 180°F in the thigh and 160°F in the stuffing.

Like a magician pulling a rabbit out of a hat, you'll reach into the oven bag and pull out your turkey—to raves from your kitchen audience.

"I turned the oven on broil for 40 minutes and then turned it down to bake. The turkey looks done. It's really brown and the bag is really inflated."

Remember, color is not an indication of doneness. Be sure to follow the instructions closely to obtain the proper end result.

The roasting times given below are less than the times included on the back of the package that your oven bag came in. Young, tender turkey cooks quickly, and it's important that you check for doneness before the end of the cooking time. Monitor closely so as not to overcook the turkey or it will be dried out.

Oven-Bag Roasting Guide		
Weight (pounds)	Unstuffed (hours)	Stuffed (hours)
10 to 18	1½ to 2	2 to 2½
18 to 22	2 to 2½	2½ to 3
22 to 24	2½ to 3	3 to 3½

Fruits, flakes, and nuts . . . some people overwork the fear factor and try to do things so precisely that they drive themselves and everyone around them crazy.

"I'm using an oven bag. Do I peel the onion before I put it in the bag? How should I cut the celery? I'm making a test turkey before Thanksgiving just to see how it goes. What's the difference between buying just a breast and buying a whole turkey? If you take the legs off, will it taste different? How do I know if I cooked it okay and it comes out right?"

"Try tasting it."

"What part should I taste?"

Here's the scary part: this was a mother who had raised teenage children . . . without calling anyone for advice!

Covered Electric Roaster

> "I should have paid more attention to my mom. And now she's gone, passed away last year, and I inherited the roaster. How do I use this thing?"
>
> Whether your latest kitchen gadget is a brand-new covered electric roaster or an heirloom roaster that belonged to your mother-in-law, you'll want to know how to achieve the best results.

For many, the covered electric roaster was one of those early appliances that made life easier in the kitchen during the holidays. This convenient freestanding unit could make a family feast come together when oven space was in high demand. It was called into action from the attic, where it had been stored following its annual appearance the previous Thanksgiving.

"Everything I read says to roast uncovered. How can I do that with this roaster?"

This roaster must be used as a unit, with the lid in place.

A turkey cooked in a covered electric roaster has less of a roasted flavor than a turkey cooked uncovered in the oven. This type of cooking unit uses steam as opposed to hot air, and it cooks the bird quickly. Turkey roasted this way has its own distinct flavor, and, for many, it's just not Thanksgiving without it. But beware: this type of cooking may not lead to that oven-browned turkey of your dreams; the bird will be pale in color unless a browning sauce is used to "paint" the breast.

"My cover won't fit the roaster with my turkey in it. Is it okay to cook even if the steam escapes? Maybe I could put duct tape around the open area. My sister said to try that. What do you think?"

"I've got one of those Nesco® roasters. I've raised a 50-pound turkey and it doesn't quite fit. Can I just put it in there anyway?"

Not a good idea. Putting an oversized bird in an electric roaster is like putting a D cup in an A bra! If the lid is not placed on it correctly, the appliance will not function as it has been designed to do. The steam will escape and the turkey will not cook properly and may even become a food-safety hazard.

- Preheat the roaster to 325°F.
- Prepare the turkey. In place of plain oil, use Browning Sauce (see below) to color the skin. Brush the sauce liberally over the entire breast area.
- Place the turkey breast-side-up on a rack. Cover the roaster and close all vents.
- Brush with the Browning Sauce once during the cooking process.
- Be sure to use a meat thermometer, as color is not an indicator of doneness. You will be deceived if you wait for this paleface to turn brown, thereby over-cooking your turkey.

ROASTING GUIDE FOR COVERED ELECTRIC ROASTER		
Weight (pounds)	Unstuffed (hours)	Stuffed (hours)
6 to 10	2 to 2½	2¼ to 3
10 to 18	2½ to 3	3 to 4
18 to 22	3 to 3½	4 to 4½

"We all need a little extra makeup at times, so this turkey needs a little extra color."

Think of it as pampering the turkey. Without the Browning Sauce you'll wind up with a paleface.

Browning Sauce

¼ cup melted butter

½ teaspoon Kitchen Bouquet,® Gravy Master,® or a similar product (or simply double the amount of paprika)

½ teaspoon paprika

- Mix together all the ingredients.

High-Heat Method

A caller with a young male voice told me he was a caterer and needed to know how long to cook a turkey. Upon questioning, he confessed that he wasn't really a caterer but more of a waiter . . . In fact he was a pledge at a fraternity at Texas A&M University and needed some directions for how to make a turkey for the frat boys—fast!

Looking for a way to speed up the cooking of your turkey? Many cooks swear by the high-heat method. If you stuff the turkey, be sure to take the end temperature of the stuffing—this is especially important with the short cooking time.

"I'm forgetful from one Thanksgiving to the next. How do I roast the turkey using the high-temperature method?"

- Preheat the oven to 450°F.
- The key element in this method is aluminum foil. Place the turkey breast-side-up in the center of a piece of foil that is two to three times the length of the turkey. Without foil and a perfectly pristine oven, you run the risk of a smoke-filled oven at the very least—and a chorus of smoke alarms announcing that dinner is ready!
- Brush or spritz the turkey with oil.
- Overlap the ends of the foil to cover the turkey (imagine crossing your arms like a genie). Overlap the sides of the foil across the top of the turkey. Do not crimp!
- Fold up the sides of the foil package to prevent the juices from running out.
- Do not crimp! Do not form an airtight seal—keep the ends open to allow the heat and the air to circulate.
- Insert a meat thermometer through the foil and into the thigh.
- Place the turkey on a rack in a shallow, open pan and roast according to the timing guide below.
- To brown, carefully peel back the foil 20 to 30 minutes before the turkey is done.

HIGH-HEAT ROASTING GUIDE		
Weight (pounds)	Unstuffed (hours)	Stuffed (hours)
10 to 18	1¾ to 2¼	2¼ to 2¾
18 to 22	2¼ to 2¾	2¾ to 3¼
22 to 24	2¾ to 3¼	3¼ to 3¾

"I want to put a cup filled with broth and herbs in the center of the cavity. Will the essence of the herbs be carried in the steam from inside out? It would be like a sauna."

The fragrance sounds great but this will amount to nothing more than aromatherapy, with no effect on the flavor of the turkey.

al fresco methods

"I'm very respectful and gentle with my turkey. You know, grilling is a labor of love."

"I'm smoking a turkey here and it is F-R-E-E-Z-I-N-G! I'm in California and it's about 55°. How long is this going to take?"

"My husband had this bright idea to keep our new gas grill free of grease, so he filled the bottom with kitty litter to absorb the drips. Guess what? Not a good idea! It clogged up everything and now it won't light. We'll have to cook the turkey on the charcoal grill, and it's been so long since we've used it I forget what to do."

"I deep-fried a turkey for the first time and it came out beautiful and was excellent. The best part was my mother-in-law's exclaiming, 'Damn! You're a good chef!' Thanks for your help. You made my day."

Outdoor cooking is as old as mankind. The sweet smell of smoke and the aroma of food cooking over a fire is romance in itself. There's something really special about cooking and eating outdoors . . . should the weather permit.

The weather does dictate much about cooking al fresco. The required cooking time could change if the thermometer dips too low, if the wind is howling, or if rain or snow enter the picture.

Early man was lucky when he stumbled across fire and first tasted roasted food. Today we have a few more outdoor cooking methods available for those who want to test their skills under the open sky.

Charcoal Grill

"Every Easter, Mother's Day, Fourth of July, Thanksgiving, and Christmas, I'm the chef. I love my grill and I cook the best turkeys on it! There's a big difference between holiday cooking and everyday cooking. I've been doing this for 15 years and love running the show for the day."

A turkey is easy to grill—and you'll get rave reviews. Prepare the turkey just as you would for regular oven roasting but do not stuff it. Stuffing may be placed in a foil pouch and placed on the grill 1 hour before the turkey is done. Spray or brush the turkey with oil to prevent the skin from drying out.

Bikini turkey

There's no end to creativity in turkey preparation, whichever cooking method you choose. One imaginative cook really took his mission to heart: with a few strategically placed pieces of aluminum foil, his turkey became a candidate for the November centerfold!

To prepare the grill:

- Place a foil drip pan in the middle of the charcoal grate. The pan should be slightly larger than the turkey so that it will catch the drippings.
- Place 25 to 30 briquettes at each of the two long sides of the drip pan.
- Light the briquettes and allow them to burn until covered with gray ash (about 30 minutes).
- Place the turkey breast-side-up on the cooking grate over the drip pan.
- Add 6 to 8 briquettes to each side every 45 to 60 minutes to maintain the cooking heat. Caution: at this point, do not add briquettes that have been infused with lighter fluid.
- Be sure to maintain a temperature of 300ºF to 350ºF within the grill.
- Use a meat thermometer to determine doneness: 180ºF in the thigh and 170ºF in the breast.

We always asked the callers what state they were calling from, and invariably they would include their city. We tended to make a mental note of where our calls were coming from. I commented to one caller from Marietta, Georgia, that I received a lot of calls from there. He replied: *"That's because we men don't know what we're doing . . . but keep a lid on it and don't tell anybody!"*

With a husky laugh, the caller added, *"I'm just playing the part of a domesticated man and the turkey* appears *to be thawed. I'm cooking for my girlfriend and her mother and I really want to impress them. Help me do a turkey on the grill. Can I stuff it?"*

Dear Marietta, Georgia: You score points for trying to impress your girlfriend and her mother with your culinary talents, but you'd lose points if you stuffed the turkey and then grilled it. Serve your stuffing as a side dish. Roast it separately in the oven, or wrap it in foil and put it on the grill for an hour.

Cooking Guide for Charcoal Covered Grill	
Weight (pounds)	Unstuffed (hours)
3 to 6 (breast only)	1½ to 2¼
6 to 9 (breast only)	2 to 3
9 to 18 (whole turkey)	2 to 3

Gas Grill

> "When I was in the Boy Scouts I used to cook. You either learned to be a good cook or learned to live with wedgies—if you weren't a good cook the guys would always yank your undies! That was years ago and I sure don't want that to happen to me now!"

Grilling outdoors on a gas grill is as simple and easy as cooking with your indoor oven. You'll need to know how many burners your grill has in order to operate it properly and to grill your turkey to perfection. When its lid is closed, the gas grill functions just like your oven.

Regardless of the type of grill you have, prepare the turkey as you would normally. Remove the neck and giblets and spritz or brush the skin with oil. Insert an oven-safe meat thermometer into the thigh and proceed as follows.

First, the turkey will need a drip pan: either place the turkey in a shallow pan and put the pan on the cooking grate, or place a foil pan under the top grate—either way, the juices need to be collected in a receptacle or you'll have a greasy mess all over your grill. Just be sure the pan isn't too large, as this will inhibit the flow of air around the surface of the turkey and increase the cooking time enormously.

"I'm not a good cook or good at math, but I was told to grill my 14-pound turkey 30 minutes per pound. Does that mean it will take 44 hours to cook?"

You'll run into trouble if you calculate the cooking time using minutes per pound—and if your math isn't good you'll either undercook or overcook the turkey!

Add some turkey sizzle to your barbecue grilling season.

Any grill master knows that to achieve grilling nirvana it's essential to take the temperature of the meat, in order to achieve the perfect end temperature. Your turkey needs to be 180°F in the thigh—the same as with indoor cooking.

"My neighbor spotted the fire and called the fire department. It was a windy day and I was using mesquite wood chips. There were some leaves blowing around the deck and some embers must have slipped through the cracks on the deck and ignited more dry leaves. Flames started shooting up through the deck. The firemen came and chopped up the deck to put the fire out. But the good news was the turkey was still wonderful and cooked just right! It really was just a minor fire, but it sure surprised my husband when he came home from work."

"Ma'am, I work for the government and operate on a 'need to know' basis. The reason I'm calling is that I need to know how to grill this 'thang' on my gas grill."

Dual-burner grill
Preheat the grill to 350°F. When the grill has reached this temperature, turn one burner off and reduce the flame to medium on the remaining burner, or to a setting that maintains a temperature of 350°F. Put the turkey over the area that is not exposed to direct heat.

Your cooking time is greatly affected by how frequently you open the lid. Keep the lid closed as much as possible: each time it is opened, hot cooking air escapes, and it will take longer to cook the turkey because the grill chamber will have to heat up again.

To promote even browning, after two-thirds of your cooking time has elapsed, rotate the turkey by a half turn. Check your meat thermometer to determine doneness.

Triple-burner grill
Follow the preparation instructions given above. Preheat the grill to 350°F. When this temperature has been reached, turn off the middle burner and control the outer burners to maintain a temperature of 350°F.

Four-burner grill
Follow the preparation instructions given above. Preheat the grill to 350°F. When this temperature has been reached, turn off both of the middle burners and control the outer burners to maintain a temperature of 350°F.

Six-burner grill
Follow the preparation instructions given above. Preheat the grill to 350°F. When this temperature has been reached, turn off any two adjacent burners and turn down the remaining burners to maintain a temperature of 350°F.

SINGLE-BURNER GRILL

A single-burner grill may require a little more finesse than a multiple-burner one. It may not be the best option for a whole turkey in the larger weight range, but you have what you have so let's get it grilled to precision as best we can.

Preheat the grill to 350°F. When this temperature has been reached, reduce the heat to a low setting. Now, here's the finesse part. Place a double-thickness piece of heavy-duty foil over half of the grill—this will help to prevent the heat from blasting the turkey and will make for a more indirect heat. Two-thirds of the way through cooking, rotate the turkey a half turn to promote even distribution of heat and color. Not hard—just a little more effort to achieve that picture-perfect turkey you've been hoping for.

"To be honest with you, I'm really not a great cook, but grilling makes me look good so people just think I know what I'm doing and then they like my cooking. It's all an illusion, with a little smoke and no mirrors!"

"What's the best thing to do?"

"Follow the directions."

"You're telling a man to follow directions? Wow!"

Follow these simple guidelines and be sure to test for doneness using a meat thermometer:

GUIDE FOR COOKING ON AN OUTDOOR GAS GRILL	
Weight (pounds)	Unstuffed (hours)
6 to 10	1¼ to 2
10 to 12	2 to 3
12 to 18	3 to 4

Water Smoker

"Replenish the wine? Oh, for the smoker . . . I thought you meant me! If I started drinking wine this early I'd be talking to the turkey and they'd have to come and take me away."

Slightly more exotic—for the adventuresome griller—is the water smoker. This is a little more work but well worth the effort. Turkey grilled on a water smoker will have dark, brownish-red skin and a reddish-pink band of color under the skin. This distinctive rosy color is a result of the meat's pigment reacting to the burning charcoal. It's normal. It's natural. It's characteristic of turkey cooked on this type of grill. Be sure to use a meat thermometer to determine doneness, as color is not an indicator.

Talk Turkey to Me

The water smoker yields a marvelously smoky-flavored turkey. And using liquids other than water, such as apple juice or wine, will enhance the aroma and the romance of cooking.

Keep in mind the following fundamental elements when using your water smoker:

- Never stuff a turkey that you plan to smoke. The lower grill temperatures used in smoking pose a food-safety risk for the stuffing.
- Use a turkey no larger than 18 pounds, in order to avoid a food-safety risk.
- The quality of your charcoal briquettes affects your cooking time, as does the weather—especially wind.
- Always use a meat thermometer to determine doneness. For food safety, the turkey must reach 140°F within 4 hours.

WATER-SMOKING GUIDE (ESTIMATED TIMES)	
8 to 12 pounds	4 to 8 hours
12 to 18 pounds	6 to 10 hours

Just allow for plenty of time—and have lots of appetizers and wine on hand for your guests. They may have a long wait until dinner!

Now, let's get cooking. The most challenging part of smoking is preparing the smoker. Follow along and be sure not to miss a step. If you can read, you can cook!

- Prepare the smoker by removing the center ring and opening all the vents.
- Place 10 pounds of briquettes in the charcoal chamber. Light the briquettes. When they're covered with gray ash (after about 30 minutes), it's time to start the smoking.
- Meanwhile, line the water pan with heavy-duty foil and put the pan in the center of the ring.
- Prepare the thawed turkey. Remove the neck and giblets and drain the juices from the body cavity. Blot the skin dry using paper towels.
- Do not stuff the turkey.
- Spritz or brush the skin liberally with oil all over.
- Insert a meat thermometer into the thigh.
- Place the center ring on the bottom section of the grill.
- Fill the water pan with hot water, apple juice, or another liquid.
- Replace the top cooking rack.
- Place the turkey on the cooking rack.
- Cover the smoker and close the vents by one-third.
- If you've made it this far, you're almost home. Just a few more essentials:
- Soak 5 chunks of hardwood in water for approximately 1 hour. This is what will produce the smoke.
- After the turkey has been cooking for about 1¼ hours, place the chunks of soaked wood on the coals.

Still with me? You're going to love the taste of this turkey! Be patient—very patient—because the turkey will be smoking anywhere from 4 to 10 hours.

The variable time is due to many factors, including the size of the turkey, the quality of the briquettes, the wind, the outdoor temperature, and how frequently you raise the lid to peek into the smoker. Given such a large timeframe, you know you'll have to add more coals to keep the fire going. So please keep following along…

- Maintain the heat of the smoker at 250°F by adding 12 to 14 briquettes every 90 minutes.
- Refill with hot water or another hot liquid as needed. To sweeten the aroma, you can use apple juice or wine—or any other liquid that strikes your fancy. But remember, the liquid must be hot when added to the water pan.

"My husband couldn't smoke the turkey on Thanksgiving because I went into labor. I had a baby boy the day after Thanksgiving. Now that I'm home, can we smoke this turkey?"

This is a great time to smoke the turkey! The many hours needed to smoke the bird will give you two a chance to relax and cuddle with your newborn. You'll have time to prepare the side dishes, change a few diapers, set the table, change a few diapers, run to the store for the requisite last-minute items, change a few diapers—and maybe even take a nap. Perfect timing!

"My wife and daughter went shopping and will be gone all day. The last time they went out they got me this water smoker, and the time before that I got socks. I've never used the smoker but I'm going to surprise them with dinner when they come home. I hate shopping but I like what they buy for me…maybe this time they'll bring me the new car I've been looking at! I can always hope!"

Deep Fryer

"Okay, I've got my HAZMAT* suit on and I'm ready to fry my turkey. How long will it take?"

* Acronym for "hazardous materials."

Deep-fried turkey is a long-time favorite, with origins in the southern states. From Texas to Louisiana to Georgia, gradually it has grown in popularity and taken hold of the Union! Everyone who has tasted deep-fried turkey raves about its tenderness, juiciness, and taste. Worrisome reports by safety experts and the potential inferno caused by backyard chefs have done little to dampen the spirit of the brave.

The method itself is simple: plunge a fully defrosted turkey into a pot of boiling oil and leave it there until cooked. However, there are numerous variables that can make this a potentially hazardous scenario. The bottom-line dangers are as follows:

- Even a turkey that is partially frozen can, when placed in 350°F oil, cause a spillover, which could ignite the propane and result in flames shooting upward. Remember, oil and water do not mix. Ever drip water into a pan of frying bacon? Picture that reaction on a much larger scale—with 5 gallons of boiling oil at your feet.
- If the pot is overfilled with oil and your fully defrosted turkey causes the oil to spill over the fryer unit, the effect will be the same. The spilt oil could well ignite the open propane. Imagine a vertical flamethrower and you have the picture.
- Currently, there are no thermostat controls on turkey fryers and the oil could overheat to the point of spontaneous combustion. Poof, you're on fire—you, and the deck, fence, house, garage, and surrounding forest or grassland.

These are but a few of the risks to your personal safety and that of your possessions. Underwriters Laboratories, Inc., safety experts, and firefighters all worry about the increased use of turkey fryers and the risks taken by consumers when using this method of cooking.

If, however, you have weighed the risks and, like most cavemen, are intrigued by backyard fires, you may wish to venture forth into the taste-tempting phenomenon of deep-fried turkey.

SAFETY TIPS
Always take the following safety precautions:

- Use your turkey fryer outdoors only, and at a safe distance from buildings, decks, and all flammable materials. Keep in mind that concrete can be stained should the oil overflow.
- Determine the exact amount of oil needed by placing your packaged turkey in the pot and filling the pot with water up to 1 or 2 inches above the turkey. Remove the turkey and note how many inches from the top of the pot the water level is: this is how many inches from the top the oil should be. Pour the water out and dry the pot thoroughly.
- Use only an oil that has a high smoking point, such as peanut, sunflower, or canola oil.

- Heat the oil to 375°F. Use a deep-fry temperature gauge or candy thermometer to accurately determine the temperature of the oil. It will take 45 to 60 minutes for the oil to reach this temperature.
- While the oil is heating up, you may inject the turkey with marinades to add flavor to the turkey.
- Use only a fresh turkey, as frozen turkeys already have a basting solution in the breast meat.
- Never stuff a deep-fried turkey.
- Once the turkey fryer is in use, never, ever leave it unattended.

"Okay, I probably should have been a little more cautious when I lowered the turkey into the oil. When it slipped off the hook and plopped into the pot, the oil slurped over the sides and onto my shoes. My shoes melted to the deck! It was an expensive dinner when you count the cost of the Nikes I had to replace, but it was the best-tasting turkey I've ever had!"

"I like living on the edge. Cooking with five gallons of hot oil, kids running, dogs chasing . . . the nearby house and wooden deck, plus a few firecrackers— ain't no better way to spend the Fourth of July!"

When the turkey fryer is in use, never let children or pets near it—or even near the frying area. Even after the turkey is done, the oil in the fryer will remain dangerously hot for a long time, continuing to pose a risk to children and pets.

"Okay, I've got my HAZMAT suit on and I'm ready to fry my turkey. How long will it take?"

Remember that earlier question? Well, here's the simple answer.

Preheat the oil to 375°F and slowly lower the turkey into the oil.

A whole turkey will take 3 minutes per pound to fry. Turkey parts, such as breasts, wings, thighs, or legs, will require 4 to 5 minutes per pound. Either way, carefully remove the turkey or the parts to test for doneness. A meat thermometer inserted into the breast should read 170°F. The temperature of legs and thighs should be 180°F.

"I'm deep-frying a turkey. When is it done? I'm waiting for it to get to 375°F and it's just not happening."

Honey, the oil needs to be at 375°F but the turkey only needs to get to 180°F in the thigh."

"Oh, I thought the turkey had to get that hot!"

"I've marinated a frozen basted turkey and I want to brine it, too, and then deep-fry it. How do I do that?"

You don't. Basted, marinated, and brined turkeys all have a water solution that is absorbed by the cells, which makes the meat juicier. This extra water in the meat just doesn't mix well with hot oil. Imagine dropping water onto a skillet that has hot oil in it. Now imagine 5 gallons of hot oil and water added to it. Always use a fresh turkey if you deep-fry, as it is all turkey without any water added.

"I'm 22 and I'm not an idiot. My turkey is completely frozen. Can I deep-fry it, like they do frozen French fries?"

Not unless you have insurance and your community has an active 911 system. Dropping a frozen turkey into oil will cause the oil to bubble up ferociously and to potentially flare up to the point of posing a fire hazard. A bad idea—even if you're 22 and not an idiot.

If you're man enough to try your hand at the holiday cooking this year, your insurance is paid up, you have excellent medical coverage through your employer, and the 911 emergency system is active in your area, you may earn yourself a merit badge for inventiveness with your new turkey fryer.

"We deep-fried the turkey for Christmas. It was delicious! But now I'm in a quandary. What do I do with all that oil? I asked my husband several times to get rid of it because it's so heavy I can't move it. It's pushing Lent already and guess what? It's still out in the garage. I suppose I'll just have to empty it one gallon at a time with an old milk jug."

Fans of deep-fried turkey can put all of that hot oil to use with some quick vegetable side dishes (see pages 105 and 128). After the turkey has been fried, it needs to rest for 20 minutes. While the oil is still hot, make the side dishes.

Post-dinner note: Once the oil has cooled, you may save it for future frying if you follow these guidelines:

- Filter the oil using a fine strainer. If the turkey or deep-fried vegetables were breaded or heavily seasoned, you may need to line the strainer with several layers of cheesecloth to catch all of the tiny particles.
- The oil should be covered and stored in the refrigerator; otherwise it may become rancid. It can be stored for several months.

- Peanut oil may be used 3 or 4 times to fry a turkey, according to the Texas Peanut Producers Board, before it begins to deteriorate. Foaming, darkening, and excessive smoking are indications that the oil should be discarded. A rancid odor and failure of food to bubble when placed in the hot oil are other signs of deterioration.

seductive favorites

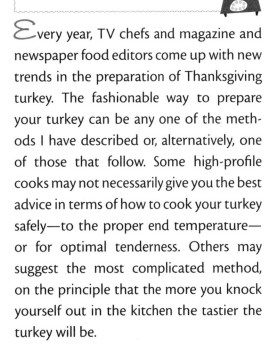

"I really want to make a statement this year. Can you tell me about brining my turkey?"

Every year, TV chefs and magazine and newspaper food editors come up with new trends in the preparation of Thanksgiving turkey. The fashionable way to prepare your turkey can be any one of the methods I have described or, alternatively, one of those that follow. Some high-profile cooks may not necessarily give you the best advice in terms of how to cook your turkey safely—to the proper end temperature—or for optimal tenderness. Others may suggest the most complicated method, on the principle that the more you knock yourself out in the kitchen the tastier the turkey will be.

But if you're tempted to try something new, go for it. Just be sure to cook your turkey to the proper end temperature, no matter how long it takes, and keep in mind the food-safety concerns covered on pages 63 to 65.

Brining

"I'm unclear on the concept but I really want to brine my turkey. My mother-in-law is on a low-sodium diet. Can I still brine it?"

Brining is simply soaking the turkey in a salt-water solution in the refrigerator. It enhances the juiciness of a fresh turkey, as the salt solution enters the cells and that is what produces the juicy taste and appearance. Many types of meat are processed with a sodium solution that increases tenderness and juiciness. If you have dietary restrictions or prefer not to process your foods, this may not be a healthy choice for you. But if the procedure for brining your turkey interests you, read on.

BASIC BRINED TURKEY
Always use a fresh turkey for brining. Frozen turkeys have their own sodium solution already added to the breast meat.

- Use 1 cup of kosher salt per gallon of water (if you substitute table salt for kosher salt, reduce it by half). You may need several gallons of salted water, depending on the size of your turkey. A 12-pound turkey will need at least 2 gallons of brine.
- Place the turkey breast-side-down in a large stockpot or food-safe plastic bag. Add the salt solution, remove all air from the bag, seal it, and place it in the stockpot, which will collect any brining solution that might seep out of the bag.
- Put the turkey in the refrigerator. The brining time will depend on the size of the turkey (see the Brining Guide at right). Rotate the turkey periodically to ensure that all parts of the bird are covered by the solution.
- When the brining is complete, remove the turkey from the solution, drain the cavity, and pat the turkey dry with paper towels. It is not necessary to rinse.

Cook the turkey using your favorite method. Stuff if desired, although the stuffing may taste saltier than usual. My experience with brining is that the skin browns unevenly and in patches, so you may not end up with a picture-perfect turkey.

Apple Cider Brine

1 cup kosher salt per gallon of liquid

1 cup brown sugar per gallon of liquid

1 gallon apple cider

6 cups water

4 apples, sliced

- Place all of the ingredients in a large stockpot. Heat thoroughly and then let cool. Place the turkey in the cooled solution and refrigerate. Follow the Brining Guide below. After brining, cook the turkey using your favorite method.

BRINING GUIDE	
Under 12 pounds	6 to 8 hours
12 to 14 pounds	12 hours
20 pounds	Up to 24 hours

Cheesecloth Method

"Do I cover it with a towel, or just what do I do with this cheesecloth thing?"

Imagine turning your turkey into a mummy. Wrapped in layers of open-weave fabric, called cheesecloth, your turkey will never achieve a crispy skin. If, however, that isn't important to you and the thought of babysitting your turkey with continual basting every 20 or 30 minutes brings you sensual delight, you've found the right method.

Six layers of cheesecloth shield the turkey just as a single layer of aluminum foil would. You must keep this "cast" moist by continually basting the turkey with the juices to prevent the cloth from sticking to the bird. With this method, the turkey will take longer to cook, because the oven door is opened and closed frequently and the oven loses heat each time. Follow the Open-Pan Roasting Guide (page 29) but add 30 to 60 minutes—perhaps more—to compensate for the reheating necessary every time the oven door is opened. It is very important that you use a meat thermometer to determine doneness.

RECYCLING QUEEN II
"I just use my husband's old white T shirts to shield the turkey during cooking, instead of cheesecloth."

$\mathcal{N}$ot an appealing thought. The mental image of those T shirts in their former life is enough to kill anybody's appetite.

One caller claimed that she lived in the same town as Martha Stewart's mother and saw her frequently. She wanted to bend the woman's ear and have her enlighten Martha. The best way to cook a turkey, the caller believed, was not to fuss with cheesecloth or stuffing under the skin, but to simply place a few slices of bacon on top of the bird and then roast it.

"My mother did that when I was a kid and I remember how my sisters and I fought over the crisp strips of bacon. Watch out for Martha's next big hit recipe!"

Brown-Paper-Bag Method

"I figure if people don't like what I'm doing they don't have to come back next year. I'm 75 and they can take it or leave it!"

The brown-paper-bag method goes back to a simpler time—and it's definitely a method that should be left behind! To bring it up to the new millennium, let's reach back to the Nancy Reagan era and the mantra "Just say NO!"

Thawing or cooking in a brown paper bag is not recommended. Today's brown bags are generally made from recycled materials, which means that chemicals have been incorporated into the paper. Therefore, heat from the oven could potentially launch a chemical assault on your turkey, rendering it unfit to eat: you and your fellow diners could be unknowingly ingesting unsafe substances. Additionally, paper tends to burn, and an impromptu turkey flambé is not the way to wow your guests. While you may hear glowing reports of how good a turkey, chicken, pheasant, or

Cornish hen tastes when roasted in a paper bag, please resist the temptation.

Low-Temperature Overnight Method

> "Last night I put my turkey in the oven for 1 hour at 500°F and then shut it off. It doesn't seem done. Can I start cooking it again?"
>
> Cooking at a low temperature is risky. Bacteria may not be killed even if you crank up the temperature and cook longer. So it's kind of like a Clint Eastwood Dirty Harry turkey—you could eat it, but how lucky do you feel?

There's a long history of low-temperature cooking, and many variations on the technique. However, this is an unsafe way to cook a turkey. Perhaps it goes back to the days of our great-grandmas, when cast-iron stoves would hold the heat for hours. Today's appliances, though, leave too much room for error. A low temperature is simply considered insufficient to kill food-borne bacteria.

"I've got this recipe that says to cook at 375°F for 1 hour, then lower the temperature to 185°F and cook until done. But that's, like, until Christmas. What do you think?"

Low-temperature cooking may sound appealing . . . time to clean the kitchen before the guests arrive, or imagine waking up to the aroma of roast turkey . . . But the thought of potential food poisoning, particularly among the young or the elderly, should convince you that this method is ill-advised.

Double Your Pleasure: Roasting Two at a Time

> "They're so cute—they look like twins! Do I have to add to the cooking time since I've got two in the oven?"
>
> There's no need to add to the cooking time. Imagine you were baking cookies: whether you had one dollop of dough or a dozen, the baking time would be the same.

Some people choose to roast two turkeys at the same time, for whatever reason: they want more drumsticks, they believe a smaller bird is more tender, they want more meat, they find two birds easier to handle, or they just have always done it that way. Yet the addition of a bird in the oven tends to lead cooks down the path of mathematical confusion. The big question seems to be the amount of time needed to roast two turkeys simultaneously. Do you add the two weights together and cook as if you had one big turkey in the oven? Do you add just a little extra time? The answer is simple: if you have two turkeys that weigh approximately the same, cook them as if you had only one, using the lower of the two weights to calculate the required roasting time.

Roast your two turkeys using the Open-Pan Roasting Guide for one turkey (page 29). Just be sure there's enough room between the two pans for the air to circulate, so that the birds will roast evenly. Simple!

Upside-Down Roasting

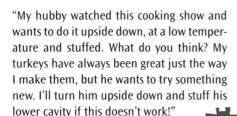

"My hubby watched this cooking show and wants to do it upside down, at a low temperature and stuffed. What do you think? My turkeys have always been great just the way I make them, but he wants to try something new. I'll turn him upside down and stuff his lower cavity if this doesn't work!"

The idea behind roasting a turkey breast-side-down is to make the juices run through the breast, bathing the meat in moisture and therefore tenderizing it. This method will always have its believers. There's no harm in trying the upside-down technique as long as you understand that the breast will most likely become smashed due to the weight of the bird. Also, the turkey will

brown unevenly in the absence of a V rack, and turning the bird so that it will brown on all sides is a hazardous undertaking. There's little meat on the back of a turkey, yet with this method the backside is what's facing up. Still, a bird can look good from the front or the back—to each his own!

Upon hearing that the breast would be smashed if the turkey were placed upside down, the caller remarked, *"No one likes a flat breast, not even the turkey. I like my breast perky!"*

Roasting from Frozen

"I really want to surprise my wife with a Christmas gift on Christmas Eve. I want to give her a frozen 16-pound turkey so she can cook it up on Christmas Day. How long will it take to cook from frozen?"

If that's your special gift to your wife, she'll be more than surprised. And she certainly will be cooking from frozen!

If you just didn't get around to thawing your turkey, you can still salvage your dinner by cooking the bird from frozen. Forget about retrieving the giblets—and don't even think about stuffing the turkey. Place the turkey on a rack and brush it with oil. Put it in a 325°F oven and plan on lots of extra roasting time. While you may have a drier-tasting turkey than you'd like, this unconventional method has saved many a cook from having to resort to tube steaks for the entrée.

"My grandkids are cooking for Thanksgiving this year and didn't know they had to thaw the turkey. Is there a quick fix? What can we do?"

It is recommended that a shallow, open pan be used to roast a turkey from frozen. Brush the skin with oil and roast uncovered for two-thirds of the cooking time. Do not baste. Then tent the breast and continue cooking until the thigh temperature reaches 180°F. Discard the neck and giblets, as they may not have reached a temperature sufficiently high to ensure food safety. Let the turkey rest for 20 minutes before carving.

"If I start cooking from frozen, do I need to drill a hole in the turkey to put the meat thermometer in?"

You may place an oven-safe thermometer in the turkey when you check it at the two-thirds point.

GUIDE FOR ROASTING FROM FROZEN	
Weight (pounds)	Roasting time (hours)
7 to 9	4 to 4½
9 to 12	4½ to 5
12 to 14	5 to 6
14 to 16	6 to 6¾
16 to 18	6¾ to 7¼
18 to 20	7¼ to 8

When told the minimum roasting time needed, the caller said, *"Oh, thanks! I'll add 2 more hours. I like the meat falling off the bone."*

To each his own . . .

Microwaving

"We just moved into a new condo last week and I told everyone I'd have Christmas here. That was good thinking…NOT! It's not going to be perfect—we've still got stuff in boxes, my oven isn't hooked up yet, and we can't have a grill on the balcony due to fire regulations. I'm a vegetarian, too, so I really don't know what to do with the turkey. Any great ideas on how to cook it without a grill or an oven?"

While most people opt for more traditional methods of preparing the star of their feast, leaving the microwave oven for the reheating of side dishes, there are times when microwaving is a convenient last resort. From the mundane ("My oven is on the blink") to the exotic ("We're sailing on our boat and we only have a microwave"), there are many reasons why people cook their turkey in the microwave.

But if you think this will be a fast and easy way to cook your turkey, think again. This intricate method will not save you much time and will require you to "babysit" your turkey. However, although microwaving a turkey requires a great deal of attention, the results are satisfying: the turkey will taste just like oven-roasted turkey. So if this is the only option available to you, feel confident that your dinner will be a resounding success.

STEPS TO SUCCESS

- Size matters, so make sure the turkey fits comfortably in the microwave. A turkey larger than 12 pounds is not recommended. If your microwave has a carousel, make sure the turkey will be able to rotate properly.
- The turkey must be completely thawed.
- You may or may not stuff the turkey.
- Microwaving will not brown the turkey beautifully, so you'll have to test your cosmetic skills. Use the simple Browning Sauce recipe on page 36 throughout the cooking process.

- Place the turkey breast-side-down in a microwavable dish. To keep the turkey level while it is upside down, put one or two wooden spoons underneath the bird to keep it from rocking and cooking unevenly. Brush the turkey with the Browning Sauce.
- Microwave on high for 4 minutes per pound. If your microwave does not have a carousel, rotate halfway through the cooking time. If your microwave has a carousel, just let it whirl!
- Turn the turkey breast-side-up and remove and discard all drippings, as they will divert microwave energy. Brush the turkey with the Browning Sauce and cook at 50 percent power for 8 minutes per pound. Divide this time into 4 quarters and follow these steps:
  1. If your microwave does not have a carousel, rotate the turkey and brush it with the Browning Sauce at each quarter.
  2. Remove and discard the drippings at each quarter.
  3. After the third quarter, it's time to begin checking the turkey and stuffing for doneness. Aim for the following temperatures using a meat thermometer or a microwave probe:
     Thigh: 180°F
     Breast: 170°F
     Stuffing: 160°F

4. As microwave ovens vary in wattage, when all of the above temperatures have been reached your turkey is done regardless of how far you are into the fourth quarter.

- Cover the turkey loosely with foil and let it rest for 20 minutes before carving. Bon appétit!

After carefully going over the copious instructions for microwaving the turkey, the caller read them back to me, then said, *"I'll have to taste it first before I give it to the dogs."*

"You're kidding?"

"No, I always fix a separate turkey for my dogs!"

Rotisserie Method

"I've got a 'mission impossible' problem. I used string to tie the turkey to the spit, but I guess I didn't do a good job. The string came loose and ignited, and the wing tips caught on fire and are flapping all over every time he makes a turn around the grill. This turkey is going to self-destruct in five seconds!"

Our ancestors caught on quickly to the benefits of roasting the catch of the day on a spit. Old cowboy movies capture the camaraderie of cooking around a campfire and the rhythmic roll of a makeshift hand crank as it slowly turns the game to roasted perfection. Today's fire connoisseur has many types of rotisserie apparatus from which to choose, each with its own unique handling features. Regardless of the style or mechanics of your rotisserie, however, there are several pointers to keep in mind.

"I used to love the old cowboy movies when I was a kid and always dreamed of calf-roping in the rodeo. But I'm a city slicker and the closest I get to that dream is grabbin' those turkey legs and lasso-ing them to that bar on my rotisserie!"

- Use a 12-pound turkey or smaller unless otherwise indicated in your instruction manual.
- Tie the legs and wings in place using wet string—to prevent any "mission impossible" situations.
- Balance the meat on the spit to avoid uneven cooking.
- Make sure the drip pan covers the length of your turkey, to prevent flare-ups. Fill the drip pan with a half inch of water.
- Use a meat thermometer to determine doneness.

Boiling or Stewing

Although not your standard fare, boiled or stewed turkey is an excellent option if a historically accurate entrée is called for, or if you need rich and tasty meat for a casserole or side-dish recipe. Simple boiled meats can be served with a delicate sauce or even as "poor man's lobster," with drawn butter and parsley.

- Use a 12-pound turkey or smaller.
- Remove the giblets and neck from the cavities and drain the turkey.
- Place the turkey breast-side-down in a 16-quart stockpot.
- Fill the stockpot with water to cover the turkey.
- Bring to a boil. This will take approximately 1 hour. Skim off and discard any brown scum (soluble protein) from the water.
- Add 1 cup of chopped celery, 1 cup of chopped onion, 1 cup of sliced carrots (optional), and several cloves of garlic, chopped (optional). Season with salt and pepper.
- Reduce the heat and simmer, uncovered, for 1½ hours or until the turkey is done.
- Remove the meat from the bones using two forks so that the meat is shredded. Use the broth that the turkey has cooked in as a sauce for the meat, or reserve it for use as a soup base.

Cooking Breast of Turkey

"Something new has happened to me. I thought I was buying a whole turkey but there aren't any wings, legs, or giblets, so I guess I picked up a breast. There aren't any instructions. How long do I cook it?"

"I'm planning a menu for a culinary arts class. How much breast meat do I need to feed 50 people?"

As a rule of thumb, purchase at least three-quarters of a pound per person. While you may pay more per pound for breast meat, you'll have less waste than with a whole turkey.

"I've just celebrated my 43rd wedding anniversary, which means that I've cooked 43 turkeys. But now I have orders from 'headquarters' to change to a breast since there are only two of us. How do you cook just a breast?"

It depends on which method you use. Whichever one you choose, initially brush the skin with oil, be sure to use a meat thermometer, look for an internal temperature of 170°F, and follow the recommended cooking times.

GUIDE FOR COOKING TURKEY BREAST (3 TO 9 POUNDS)		
Open pan	1½ to 2¾ hours	325°F
Convection oven	1¼ to 2¼ hours	325°F
Oven bag	1¼ to 1¾ hours	350°F
Outdoor grill	1½ to 2½ hours	Indirect/medium heat/350°F

"I'm 84 years old and I'm only going to cook a breast this year because everyone else is dead . . . not from my cooking, mind you!"

Crock-Pot Method

"I live in an apartment and my oven hasn't worked for seven years. It's no big deal because my landlord gives me a break on the rent. I usually use my crock pot to cook my meals. Can I cook turkey in one?"

The crock pot is a way for busy people to have a great meal at the end of the day without any stress. I suggest choosing a breast as opposed to a whole turkey, and it should be no more than 5½ to 6 pounds.

Brush the skin with butter. Sprinkle with seasonings such as oregano, basil, and/or tarragon. Add 2 tablespoons of chopped fresh parsley. Sprinkle with paprika, salt, and pepper. Add ¼ to ½ cup of liquid such as water, sherry, or wine. Cook on high for 1 hour, then reduce the heat to low and cook for 6 to 7 hours.

Be sure to use a meat thermometer to determine doneness. Anywhere from 30 to 60 minutes before you expect the meat to be done, begin checking for an internal temperature of 170°F. Let the turkey rest for 20 minutes before carving.

"My wife says that I don't appreciate her so I have to cook the turkey this year. She says that I work all the time, leave her and the kids, and don't value all the work involved in getting a dinner ready. So she's thrown down the gauntlet and I'm rising to the challenge."

Tender, juicy, perfectly prepared turkey is the star attraction any time of year.

Talk Turkey to Me

can we talk? when the road to culinary delight gets rocky

Cooking Interruptus: Dealing with Power Failures and Traveling with Turkeys

"We just moved into our new home and the oven doesn't work. The oven man came out to fix it but told us he couldn't because the problem was with the gas-line pressure. This is a brand-new house! We've got to get hold of the gas company, but how am I going to cook this turkey right now?"

It may be that the electricity cuts out due to a sudden snowstorm or an unpaid bill. Or worse yet, a whole grid system goes down. (Once, the entire eastern grid of the United States failed, causing a huge blackout!) Or perhaps the gas line ruptures down the street and you're right in the middle of cooking your holiday feast. Flashlights and candles can be fun, but they won't cook a big turkey in time for dinner.

"I've been cooking for years, but this year the potential in-laws are coming for dinner. Well, they're not really 'potential' in-laws any more—they'll be real in-laws very soon. I have a potential grandchild on the way!"

Some things you just can't plan for!

While there are some things you can't plan for, you can always deal with a power failure by resorting to plan B. Think of it as survival training—your American duty to cope with the unforeseen. Your readiness to meet the challenge head-on will stave off an impending disaster. And by keeping a positive outlook and enlisting the help of all hands, you'll pull together a group of unwitting volunteers and get the job done. And one thing you can count on is having a truly memorable meal!

"We're right in the middle of cooking our turkey and the electricity has gone out. What do I do now?"

With power failures, you have to think outside the box and come up with alternative sources of fuel. Consider the various methods included in this book. If the gas has been cut, cook your turkey using electric heat—crank up that microwave, or borrow an electric roaster. If the power is out and you don't have a gas oven, take to the grills—grab some charcoal briquettes or fire up the gas grill. This may be the year you try deep-fried turkey! A little American ingenuity and creativity will get you through it. If all else fails, dig into those stowed-away wedding gifts in search of the ubiquitous fondue pot that's never been used. You can do this!

"I've got Thanksgiving blessings: I live on the Snake River in Idaho—it has a beauty all its own—the grandchildren are coming, and nothing could be better!"

"Over the river and through the woods to Grandmother's house we go." That's how the old song begins. Packing the kids and the turkey into the car is a holiday tradition for many Americans. The image of Grandma's tranquil Idaho home does not correlate with the scene of pandemonium as the family takes to the highway in order to get there. Traveling with the kids, the pets, and the turkey simply adds to the stress of the day. But without at least a modicum of commotion, it would hardly be a holiday at all!

"Dad is 87 and wants Christmas at his home. He doesn't cook, so you have to bring half the house with you when you go. Everyone literally has to travel 'over the river and through the woods' to get there—and he's 6 hours away! I'm bringing the turkey and think of it more as bringing a sacrificial offering to the powers that be."

Before you take your turkey on that infamous one-way ride, decide whether you'll be preparing it at home and taking it ready to eat or cooking it at your destination. There are several things to consider, the most obvious being the number of hours it will take to reach your destination. Keep in mind that your prepared turkey must be refrigerated within 2 hours of being cooked or it could pose a safety hazard.

According to the number crunchers at the Centers for Disease Control and Prevention, in the United States alone there are now more than 173,000 cases of food-borne illness annually. Many of those cases are a result of eating restaurant food, but some are caused by poor food handling in the home. One of the main causes of food poisoning is improper cooking practices—failure to cook food to the temperature needed to kill bacteria within 4 hours or failure to cook to the end temperature needed to kill bacteria. Another significant factor in food-borne illness is the time elapsed between preparation and serving; in other words, the time between oven and table should be carefully monitored. Symptoms of food-borne illness include headaches, muscle aches, diarrhea, dizziness, and vomiting.

⊚

A pilot, copilot, and the copilot's wife had just sat down to dinner when the pilot received a call. They had to fly to Wichita to pick up a donated liver.

"Can we hold the turkey 4 hours until they get back?"

In cases such as this, it's best to carve the turkey, then sprinkle the slices with pan juices or broth and refrigerate. When you're ready to eat, simply reheat in a covered, oven-safe dish in a 350ºF oven for at least 30 minutes.

⊚

"We've got a situation here. The Santa Barbara winds blew the power lines down and we're only halfway through cooking. The turkey has been out of the oven for about an hour. What should we do?"

If you have a grill, get it going immediately and continue cooking the turkey until it's done. It will take longer than you think: you just don't pick up cooking where you left off; the turkey must first heat through to the temperature it had reached when the power went off, then continue to cook for the recommended time.

If a gas or charcoal grill is not an option, immediately plunge the turkey into ice and store it in an ice chest until the power returns. But don't delay. Time is of the essence!

One wise guy joked that sometimes he just needed to have some "bad food" to clean out his system. Somehow, eating a salad seems a better way to clean out your system!

If you'll be arriving within 2 hours and then eating immediately, simply wrap the turkey in layers of foil topped by layers of cloth (towels, blankets, etc.) to hold in the heat. If possible, place the bird in an insulated chest. Carve it immediately upon arrival.

⊚

Should your timeframe expand—say, you want to visit with your family and friends before sitting down to eat—it will be necessary to handle your cooked turkey differently. When it's not feasible for you to reach your destination or to eat within a safe timeframe, it's better to exercise caution.

"It was raining this morning when we got up, so my husband's golf game got cancelled. This, then, was going to be our little 'together' day. So this afternoon I put the turkey on for dinner and at about four o'clock the sun came out and one of the 'boys' called to quickly get some golf in, and off he went. So I'm spending my day with the other turkey . . . How can I keep it warm until the big turkey gets back?"

If it will be only 1 or 2 hours until dinner, keep the turkey warm by wrapping it in foil and perhaps a towel for added insulation. If it will be more than 2 hours, it's best to follow the advice given to the copilot's wife: carve the meat, sprinkle with pan juices or broth, refrigerate, and then reheat later.

Cooking at High Altitudes

"We're all high in Colorado. We just don't know *how* high!"

"We're having a family reunion at a chalet in the Rockies this year. My brother has a place near Breckenridge and we'll be at 8,600 feet. What changes do I need to make in cooking?"

There are many answers to this question —and several of them are contradictory. I surfed the Web for an answer and found one source that recommended adding 5 to 10 minutes per pound when cooking at high altitudes! Do not do this!

According to the Colorado State University Cooperative Extension, there's no need to adjust times for roasting or grilling a turkey at high altitudes. But if you're deep-frying your turkey, it's recommended that you lower the temperature of the oil by 3°F for every 1,000 feet in elevation, to avoid over-browning the outside while undercooking the inside. If you're using an oven cooking bag, you could make two or three additional slits. Regardless of the method you choose, it's absolutely essential that you use a meat thermometer to determine doneness and that you make sure your oven is calibrated properly.

These guidelines do not apply to the side dishes of the meal. The cooking times for baked items and vegetable dishes may be different, as altitude affects leavening and the boiling of water (water boils at a lower temperature at high elevations). On its Web site, the Colorado State University Cooperative Extension will answer your questions about high-altitude cooking (www.ext.colostate.edu).

Food Safety Made Simple

"We're not even good cooks, let alone worry about whether it's safe!"

Both good cooks and not-so-good cooks should be concerned about food safety. Unsafe food can make you ill with fever, diarrhea, or stomach cramps and even put you in the hospital. Food safety is something many people take for granted, believing that the items they purchase are free from the beasties that cause food poisoning. In reality, however, bacteria are naturally present in meat and poultry.

"We'll have to give our turkey a Pap test to determine if there's bacteria."

If only it were that easy. In fact, you can't even see or smell the toxins.

The caller said he had smoked his turkey on Sunday and held it warm in the oven on Monday and Tuesday. This was Wednesday and he wasn't sure it was done—could he reheat it?

"Let me get this straight. You prepared your turkey on Sunday and it hasn't seen the inside of a refrigerator for 3 days? Do you have 911 on speed dial?"

"Can I give it to the dog?"

"How much do you like your dog—or your carpet?"

"I'm having an emotional problem . . . my emotions, not the turkey's—he's beyond emotion. The pressure is on to cook, be safe, and be ready on time. My concern is, I have to cook the turkey before work and the Brownie Scouts party isn't until after school. That would be bad form—to poison 10 Brownies at our meeting after school . . . if someone gets sick I'll never get invited back to be a troop leader!"

Here are some unsanitary practices that can lead to rapid bacterial growth:

- thawing meat or poultry at room temperature
- splashing raw meat or poultry juices around the sink and counter—this can lead to cross-contamination of other foods
- cooking at a low temperature so that the food does not reach the critical temperature needed to prevent the growth of food organisms
- undercooking meat or poultry
- stuffing the turkey the night before cooking it
- leaving cooked meat out on the counter (unrefrigerated) for more than 2 hours

"So if I've done something wrong, what happens? Do I go to the penalty corner, or what?"

You must assume the responsibility for illness when you push the boundaries of food safety.

"I run a non-profit center and I don't want the headlines to read, 'Closed due to food poisoning'!"

So what can you do to make sure your celebration is a happy and healthy one?

"I hear so many things can go wrong. You start with a good turkey and something you do makes it go bad. Sounds like a spring-break horror movie: **When Good Turkeys Go Bad!"**

Whether you're serving turkey, ham, or any other meat, keep the following steps in mind:

- Thaw in the refrigerator or in cold water. If thawing in the refrigerator, place the meat on a tray to collect any juices that may drip.
- Wash surfaces with warm, soapy water or a mild bleach solution to prevent cross-contamination of other foods. A homemade solution consisting of 1 tablespoon of bleach to 1 gallon of water is easy, economical, and effective.

- If you decide to stuff the turkey, do so just before roasting.
- Never cook meat at a temperature lower than 325°F.
- Use a meat thermometer to determine doneness.
- Refrigerate leftovers within 2 hours. It's best to remove the stuffing and the meat from the carcass, wrap it, and store it in small or medium-sized containers to promote quick chilling down to 40°F.
- To minimize the risk of food-borne illness, keep hot foods hot and cold foods cold. Hot means over 140°F and cold means at or below 40°F. The range between is perfect for brewing a bacterial stew!

"I've cooked my 10-pound turkey at 325°F for 6 hours. Do I need to cook it another hour to be safe?"

"No, don't worry about it. You've overcooked your turkey by 3 hours. You're definitely safe, but the turkey will probably be very dry."

"Oh, that's okay. We'll just put a lot of cranberry sauce over it."

There's a happy medium between food safety and food that is cooked to the proper end temperature so that it's succulent and tasty. However, there are preferences in everything . . .

"My husband is going in for surgery and I'm cooking his favorite meal. Turkey. Dry."

"Oh, you mean well done?"

"No, dry . . . And that's pretty hard to do since he likes his steaks rare. But he had salmonella once and never wants it again, so I overcook the turkey by 2 hours just to get it the way he likes it."

"We let the turkey sit out overnight by accident. Can we still eat it? How sick would we get if we ate it?"

Let's put it in another context. If you went to a restaurant and you knew they had left your food out of the refrigerator overnight, would you eat it?

now, let's really talk turkey

Time to Pull It All Off: Planning Your Menu

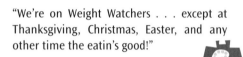

"We're on Weight Watchers . . . except at Thanksgiving, Christmas, Easter, and any other time the eatin's good!"

Planning your menu can be a challenge, but in reality this can also be a simple process. Your dinner will include an entrée, several side dishes, and dessert. Simple. The larger the gathering, the more portions you'll serve and the more side-dish and dessert options you'll need. The idea is to prepare as much as possible in advance so your day will be stress-free and you'll be able to enjoy your guests.

The key to successful entertaining is to develop your own personal style. A casual buffet or family-style dinner may suit your taste, or you may prefer the elegance of formally prepared dishes that are plated and then served to your guests.

The most important thing to remember is that no matter what you prepare or how you serve it, time spent building and rekindling relationships is what makes a celebration successful and memorable.

You may choose to slice your turkey at the table in front of your salivating guests, or in the privacy of your kitchen so no one has to witness you wrestling the legs off the bird! There's no right or wrong way—only your way. You're the conductor of this event. You orchestrate the day's festivities.

The majority of dinner gatherings revolve around either a buffet or a family-style meal with everyone seated at the table. You're the four-star general who rallies the troops for Turkey Day! Divide and conquer by having your guests take part in the food preparation. Dishes that can be made ahead and heated before serving are easy assignments for those diners who are eager to get involved. Don't feel that you're the only person who can make this dinner a success. Learning to delegate is a life skill, whether at work or at play.

"Here's what I want. I want beautifully browned turkey that's simple to prepare with all the fixins and time to enjoy myself that day."

❧

One trick of the trade is to include prepared or frozen foods as a way of simplifying last-minute preparations. Even the finest restaurants do it. Culinary shortcuts abound in grocery stores today. Bagged salad greens, frozen vegetables, and delicious pies and cakes are readily available to lighten your load. Pick up a side dish from your favorite gourmet shop. Rejoice in the blessings of this freedom! Celebrate your newfound confidence and the lack of restrictions when it comes to choosing those products or services that will help you synergize random elements into a blockbuster event.

Build your dinner menu by selecting from among the following options. The key to using these combinations successfully is to view them as merely a springboard. They're not etched in granite. Choose the side dishes that appeal to you, add an appetizer, drop a dessert—select what you think your guests will like and what you feel confident in preparing.

MENU GUIDE FOR 4 TO 6 PERSONS	
Without leftovers:	4 to 6-pound turkey breast
With leftovers:	6 to 9-pound turkey breast or whole turkey
	Appetizer
	Vegetable or salad
(seasonal option)	Cranberry side dish
	Potatoes and/or stuffing
	Gravy
	Bread or rolls
	Dessert

MENU GUIDE FOR 8 TO 12 PERSONS	
Without leftovers:	8 to 12-pound turkey
With leftovers:	12 to 18-pound turkey
	Appetizer #1
	Appetizer #2
	Vegetable or salad #1
	Vegetable or salad #2
(seasonal option)	Cranberry side dish
(optional)	Stuffing
(optional)	White potato dish
	Sweet potato dish
	Gravy
	Assorted breads/rolls
	Dessert #1
	Dessert #2

For a large group, prepare multiple side dishes in ample quantities. There are several creative ways to prepare large quantities of turkey for a crowd while still keeping production manageable.

- 1 (12-pound) turkey in the oven and
  1 (12-pound) turkey on the grill

OR

- 1 (20-pound) turkey and a 6 to 9-pound turkey breast (or other meat)

OR

- 2 (12-pound) turkeys roasted simultaneously (if they fit in your oven)

MENU GUIDE FOR 14 TO 18 PERSONS	
Without leftovers:	14 to 19-pound turkey
With leftovers:	22 to 27-pound turkey
	Appetizer #1
	Appetizer #2
	Salad
	Vegetable #1
	Vegetable #2
(seasonal option)	Cranberry side dish
(optional)	Stuffing
	White potato dish
	Sweet potato dish
	Gravy
	Assorted breads/rolls
	Dessert #1
	Dessert #2
	Dessert #3

MENU GUIDE FOR 20 OR MORE PERSONS	
Without leftovers:	20-pound turkey (or larger)
With leftovers:	30-pound turkey
	Appetizer buffet (3 or more choices)
	Salad
	Vegetable #1
	Vegetable #2
(seasonal option)	Cranberry side dish
(optional)	Stuffing
	White potato dish
	Sweet potato dish
	Gravy
	Assorted breads, rolls, and muffins
	Dessert #1
	Dessert #2
	Dessert #3
(optional)	Dessert #4

Talk Turkey to Me

Carving

"My husband and I were married for years when he ran off with a millionaire lady. This is the first turkey I'll have ever carved. Carving was always his job but now I've got to do it in front of everyone. My adult son doesn't want to do it."

"Since it's your first time carving, why not do it in the kitchen and serve the slices on a platter?"

"Oh, I never thought of that. Thank you!"

The Thanksgiving image that speaks to us from the food and cooking magazines is Norman Rockwell's timeless painting *Freedom from Want,* with everyone at the table focused on each other as the turkey is presented. It's a heartwarming scene frozen in time. If it were a celluloid work, the next frame would be the carving of the turkey. The bird would be expertly carved to the delight of the assembled diners. Some cooks feel the need to present the feast to their guests in this fashion, while others grapple with the bird well out of sight! There's no right or wrong way. Each family has its own customs and traditions.

Carving the turkey is the moment of consummation. It's what everyone's been waiting for, the true measure of your kitchen prowess. But the turkey will be just hacked away at if you don't know what you're doing!

"I'm 70 years old and cooking turkey for the first time. I was in the hospitality industry, so I always had to work holidays and never had to cook. I'm retired now and I need directions on how to carve this thing."

Carving is a simple matter, whether you decide to do it at the table under the watchful eye of your guests or in the privacy of your kitchen. There are several straightforward steps to be taken as you advance beyond Carving 101.

"I'm in the meat cutters' union, and the way I like to tackle the turkey is to put on a pair of latex gloves and just break the joints and pull the meat off the bones. Then I shred it with a fork and pour the juices over the meat. I think it tastes better that way, all shredded and loose."

"After cooking, let it rest for 20 minutes."

"What, me rest!"

"No, the turkey! You might need to rest, too, but the turkey definitely needs to rest before being carved. Imagine—it has been working hard doing all that cooking!"

- After cooking the turkey, let it rest for 20 minutes to allow the juices to set. This will make for easier slicing. If you slice too soon, the meat will shred rather than slice.

- First, remove the drumstick. Hold the end of the leg and use the tip of a sharp knife to poke into the joint connecting the leg to the body. Then dislodge the leg. *(See diagram 1 below.)*
- Next, make a large horizontal cut in the breast meat. This will ensure that the sliced portions fall away easily as you carve. *(See diagram 2 below.)*

- Slicing downward, cut through the breast meat using smooth, even strokes. Continue slicing in this manner. *(See diagram 3 and 4 below.)*
- Arrange the slices on a platter. Place the legs, thighs, and wings on the platter for those who like to gnaw on bones.

1

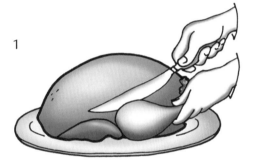

2

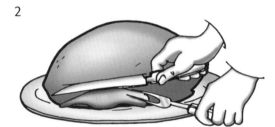

3

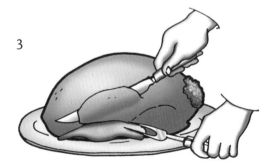

4

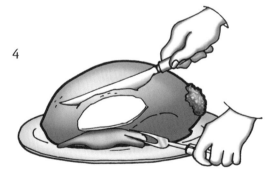

Talk Turkey to Me

Gravy

> "Mom always made the gravy and she had great success, but I can't seem to get my gravy right. Mom's in Milwaukee and I wish I could just whisk her down here. But since I can't, how do I make the best gravy?"

"My mother always seemed to overcook the turkey. It was always really dry. Matter of fact, I was 20 before I realized that gravy wasn't a beverage."

Gravy has indeed covered the sins of many a cook. It has also been a sinner itself. Lumpy. Tasteless. Too thick or too thin. The art of gravy-making has left some cooks out on a turkey limb!

Homemade pan gravy is easy to make and well worth the effort. You'll always have enough gravy if you keep a few ingredients on hand and follow these simple instructions.

HOMEMADE PAN GRAVY

You really don't need all that fat to get flavorful gravy, so skim the fat from the pan drippings using a spoon or a gravy separator.

- Stir the browned bits remaining in the bottom of the pan into a savory concoction that captures all of the flavors of the pan. Add ¼ cup of water to facilitate pouring.
- Strain this liquid and transfer it to another saucepan.
- Add enough broth or water to make 2 cups and bring to a boil. You may double or triple the recipe as desired. For every additional cup of water, add 1 chicken bouillon cube.
- Season with a sprinkling of dried basil.
- Add salt and pepper to taste.
- In a separate container, place 2 tablespoons of cornstarch and just enough water to make a liquid about the consistency of Elmer's® glue. Whisk the liquid into the saucepan and stir until it begins to boil. Reduce the heat and simmer for 1 minute or until the gravy is thickened and has a sheen to it.

LOW-CARB FLOURLESS AU JUS

Follow the instructions for Basic Pan Gravy but omit the cornstarch. Simmer for 15 minutes or until reduced by one-quarter. The gravy will be thin yet flavorful and ideal for gluten-sensitive or low-carbohydrate diners. Season with salt and pepper and, if desired, a sprinkling of dried basil.

> "Skim the fat from the gravy? But that's what makes it taste so good."

"How about putting a little wine in the cavity? How about putting a little wine in the gravy? Hmmm . . . how about putting a little wine in the cook!"

You go, girl!

If you don't have drippings to make gravy, or if you just want to try a sensational flavor burst with every bite, you'll enjoy this simple solution.

Apricot Amaretto Sauce

Makes about 2 cups

2 tablespoons butter

1 (18-ounce) jar apricot jam

¼ cup amaretto liqueur

- Melt the butter. Add the jam and allow it to melt into the butter. Add the amaretto and blend in. Simmer for 5 minutes.

"Mama! Where did you get all this gravy?"

"I told them I made it, but I had a little help from a friend. I'm a 21st-century great-grandma from North Carolina and I just used a mix."

True confessions help to alleviate the stress of the day. You don't have to do it all, as the magazines imply. And you don't have to give away your trade secrets, either. Even the finest restaurants use prepared foods in some form or fashion. So go ahead and tell them you made it—it's true, you did!

"You work like crazy for the two weeks before and then it's all gone in 15 minutes!"

TURKEY AND ALL THE TRIMMINGS
SPRING–SUMMER

Create a summer splash at your next barbecue by serving a grilled turkey
garnished with refreshing citrus fruits.

Spinach Salad with Strawberries (page 90).

Top: Sliced breast of turkey with Apricot Amaretto Sauce (page 72), Wild Rice and Mushroom Bake (page 136), Green Beans with Bacon and Blue Cheese (page 108), and Fresh Fruit Salad with Glaze (page 97).
Bottom: Raspberry-Lemon Marbled Pound Cake (page 160).

Celebrate any season with flair and flavor. A delectable platter of tender, sliced roast turkey breast (page 56) in the midst of Green Beans with Bacon and Blue Cheese (page 108), Wild Rice and Mushroom Bake (page 136), Fresh Fruit Salad with Glaze (page 97), The Ultimate Cream Cake (page 164), sliced French Onion Bread with butter pats (page 140), and Apricot Amaretto Sauce (page 72).

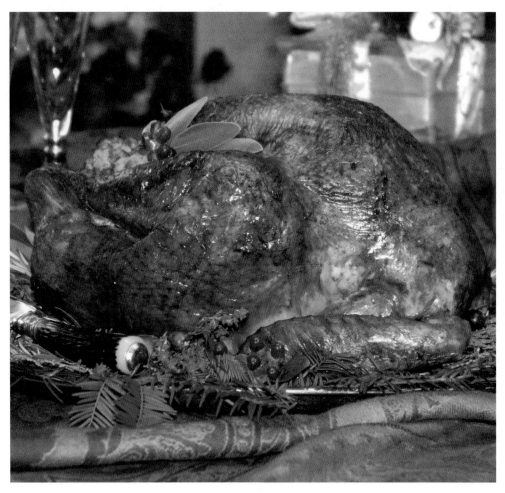

A classic holiday favorite—this perfect festive turkey with all the trimmings wouldn't be complete without friends and family around it.

Potato Gratin (page 124).

Top (left to right): Pumpkin Pie (page 149), Southern Pecan Pie (page 148),
and Apple Crostata (page 150).
Bottom: Dark Chocolate Cake with Decadent Chocolate Mousse Frosting (page 156).

A Thanksgiving tradition: tender and juicy roast turkey, Whipped Sweet Baby Carrots (page 114), Homemade Pan Gravy (page 71), Apple, Sausage, and Herb Stuffing (page 134), Cranberry Sauce (page 93), and To-Die-For Cheese Biscuits (page 143).

table talk...
let the feast begin

Whatever the season or the occasion, food brings people together. The impression has been cast by a Madison Avenue advertising agency: folks gathered harmoniously around a bountiful table. With this image comes the expectation that a feast will be perfectly prepared and presented to an assembly of expectant diners. Working women and men, stay-at-home moms, grandmothers, newlyweds, recently widowed men, and anyone who never so much as picks up a cookbook, no matter what the season, have to live up to this expectation. They feel the weight of the entire holiday feast resting squarely on their shoulders!

The pressure to prepare a juicy, tender, golden-brown turkey and all of its accompaniments, and get it all on the table while still piping hot, can lead to a deer-in-the-headlights look on the face of all but the heartiest of souls. Even if you have the time to read magazines filled with new recipe ideas, you may be reluctant to jeopardize your holiday meal with dishes that could prove difficult to prepare. Not to worry. The following tried-and-true menu suggestions could well become staples of your holiday menu. They are real recipes from real people that really work.

For those who are unsure about their talents in the kitchen, a brief word of encouragement: If you can read, you can cook. A recipe is a guide. Simply follow along. Everyone has to start somewhere. It might as well be here!

appetizers

Meant as a way to whet the appetite, the appetizer course also serves as a kick-off to the meal. Guests gather and mingle to catch up on news about family, friends, the workplace, sports, and any milestone events that have taken place since the last gathering.

When considering your culinary presentations, the most important thing to keep in mind is how much time you have. Don't overburden yourself with complicated recipes that tie you down in the kitchen. The following tempting tidbits have been chosen not only for their taste and simplicity but also because they can be prepared in advance, giving you all the more time to welcome your guests.

Hot Artichoke and Crabmeat Dip (page 80).

bacon-wrapped water chestnuts

Makes about 45 bite-sized pieces

THIS CROWD-PLEASING DISH CAN BE ASSEMBLED, COOKED, AND PLACED IN A CASSEROLE DISH A DAY IN ADVANCE. KEEP REFRIGERATED IF MAKING AHEAD.

Preheat the oven to 350°F.

Wrap a narrow strip of bacon around each water chestnut and secure with a toothpick. Place on a baking sheet and broil until the bacon is done.

Mix the brown sugar and ketchup together. Transfer the prepared water chestnuts to an oven-safe casserole dish and cover with the ketchup mixture.*

Bake, uncovered, for 30 minutes or until bubbly.

At this point the dish may be refrigerated for up to 2 days. If chilled, it will require an additional 15 minutes of baking.

1 pound bacon cut in half lengthwise and then cut in half crosswise

4 (8-ounce) cans whole water chestnuts, drained

Toothpicks to assemble

½ cup brown sugar

½ cup ketchup

hearty meatballs

Makes about 60 bite-sized meatballs

GAME DAY OR HOLIDAY, THESE MEATBALLS ARE A FABULOUS TREAT. YOU CAN MAKE THE BASIC MEATBALLS AHEAD AND THEN FREEZE THEM, EITHER FOR SEVERAL DAYS OR FOR LONG-TERM STORAGE.

THE SECRET TO THEIR LIP-SMACKING TASTE IS THE SAUCE. IT'S A SIMPLE COMBINATION THAT WILL LEAVE PEOPLE INCREDULOUS WHEN YOU TELL THEM WHAT HAS GONE INTO IT.

Preheat the oven to 450°F.

Combine all the meatball ingredients and blend well. Using a rounded teaspoon, form 60 bite-sized meatballs. Place in a shallow baking pan and bake for 15 minutes or until heated through.

To prepare the sauce, combine the chili sauce and grape jelly in a saucepan. Heat until the jelly is melted.

Place the well-drained meatballs in a serving dish and pour the sauce over them. Stir gently to coat. Serve warm.

MEATBALLS

1½ pounds lean ground beef

⅔ cup dry breadcrumbs

¼ cup water

1 egg, beaten

3 tablespoons minced onion

1 clove garlic, minced

½ teaspoon salt

¼ teaspoon pepper

Toothpicks for serving

SAUCE

1 cup chili sauce

1 cup grape jelly

deviled eggs

Makes 2 dozen

Remove the egg yolks from the whites and place in a small bowl. Mash with a fork. Add the mayonnaise, sour cream, mustard, Worcestershire sauce, salt, and hot pepper sauce. Blend until fluffy. Add the chopped dill pickle and mix well.

Mound a small scoop of the yolk mixture into the hollow of each half egg white. Arrange on a platter and sprinkle with paprika.

Cover and refrigerate until ready to serve (up to 4 hours).

12 hard-cooked eggs, peeled and halved lengthwise

3 tablespoons mayonnaise

1 tablespoon sour cream

1 tablespoon yellow mustard

1 teaspoon Worcester sauce

¼ teaspoon salt (or to taste)

⅛ teaspoon hot pepper sauce (or to taste)

1 to 2 tablespoons chopped dill pickle (to taste)

Paprika

brie with apricot preserve

Serves 12

SHORT ON TIME AND ENERGY BUT LONG ON DESIRE TO SERVE AN ELEGANT APPETIZER? THIS RECIPE IS SO EASY AND SO TASTY YOU'LL WANT TO MAKE IT ANY TIME OF THE YEAR.

Preheat the oven to 300ºF. Line a baking sheet with foil.

Cut out a circle from the top rind of the Brie, leaving a half-inch border of rind. (Remove the circle of rind.)

Place the wheel of Brie on the prepared baking sheet. Spread the apricot preserve over the Brie. Bake until the cheese is soft (about 12 minutes).

1 wheel Brie 8 inches in diameter

1 (8-ounce) jar apricot preserve

Crusty bread, assorted crackers, or apple and pear slices for serving

garlic-herbed cream cheese

Makes about 3 cups

ORDINARY CREAM CHEESE IS TRANSFORMED INTO A DELICIOUS SPREAD TO SERVE WITH A CRUSTY BAGUETTE, ASSORTED CRACKERS, AND BREADSTICKS, OR TO ADD A DELECTABLE FLAVOR TO MASHED POTATOES.

NOTE: THIS SPREAD MAY BE PREPARED IN ADVANCE AND STORED IN THE REFRIGERATOR FOR UP TO 4 WEEKS IF SEALED IN AN AIRTIGHT CONTAINER.

Blend the butter and cream cheese in a food processor until smooth and fluffy, frequently stopping the motor to scrape the sides. Add the garlic, oregano, basil, dill, marjoram, thyme, and pepper and continue to beat until well combined.

Place in a covered container and refrigerate for at least 12 hours, to allow the flavors to mellow.

8 ounces whipped butter

2 (8-ounce) packages cream cheese, softened

2 cloves garlic

½ teaspoon oregano

½ teaspoon basil

¼ teaspoon dill

¼ teaspoon marjoram

¼ teaspoon thyme

¼ teaspoon black pepper

five-layer garlic-and-cream-cheese spinach spread

Serves 12 to 15

THIS SPREAD MUST BE MADE 1 TO 2 DAYS IN ADVANCE TO ALLOW THE FLAVORS TO MELLOW AND THE MOLD TO SET. SERVE WITH CRUSTY BREAD OR ASSORTED CRACKERS.

In a bowl, mix the cream cheese, melted butter, and milk.

In a separate bowl, mix the spinach, parsley, olive oil, garlic, basil, and Parmesan cheese.

To assemble:

- Line a cake pan with plastic wrap.
- Spread one-third of the cream cheese mixture over the lined cake pan. (This should be your best-looking layer, as it will become the top layer of the dip.)
- Spread half of the spinach mixture over the cream cheese layer.
- Spread one-third of the cream cheese mixture over the spinach layer.
- Spread the remaining spinach mixture over the cream cheese layer.
- Spread the remaining cream cheese mixture over the spinach layer.

Cover and refrigerate overnight. When ready to serve, invert the pan onto a serving dish and remove the plastic wrap.

2 (8-ounce) packages cream cheese

¼ cup melted butter

2 tablespoons milk

1 (10-ounce) package chopped frozen spinach (thawed and with the water squeezed out)

1 cup chopped parsley*

¼ cup olive oil

2 garlic cloves, minced

1 teaspoon basil

1 cup grated Parmesan cheese

*Parsley is easily chopped in a food processor. Using the steel blade, whirl until chopped. If not using a food processor, use scissors to quickly snip the parsley.

easy-to-prepare appetizer buffet with delightfully delicious dill dip

Makes about 2 cups

SHOW OFF SEASONAL VEGETABLES BY SLICING AND ARRANGING THEM ON PLATTERS OR CAKE PLATES OR IN LARGE BOWLS, ALONG WITH A TASTY DIP SERVED IN A TRIMMED SWEET PEPPER OR A HOLLOWED-OUT CABBAGE. THE DIP RECIPE CAN EASILY BE DOUBLED, TRIPLED, OR QUADRUPLED BUT THE DIP SHOULD BE MADE WELL IN ADVANCE AND THEN CHILLED.

Wash and prepare all the vegetables a day in advance and refrigerate. Assemble the buffet 30 to 45 minutes before your guests are due to arrive.

To prepare the dip, chop the green onions in a food processor. Add the cream cheese and blend. Add the mayonnaise and continue to blend. Add the dill and parsley and mix until well blended.

Allow the flavors to mellow in the refrigerator for at least 4 hours before serving.

VEGETABLE SUGGESTIONS

Broccoli or cauliflower flowerets; red, green, and yellow sweet peppers; cherry tomatoes; zucchini slices or sticks; endives; carrots; cucumbers; green onions; celery stalks; sugar snap peas

DIP

2 green onions

1 (8-ounce) package cream cheese, softened

8 ounces mayonnaise

2 heaping tablespoons dried dill

2 tablespoons chopped parsley

hot artichoke and crabmeat dip

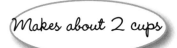

Makes about 2 cups

THIS RICH AND DELECTABLE HOT DIP IS EASY TO ASSEMBLE IN ADVANCE. SIMPLY REFRIGERATE, THEN BAKE BEFORE SERVING.

Preheat the oven to 350°F.

Thoroughly mix all the ingredients together. Pour into a greased 1-quart baking dish and bake, uncovered, for 20 minutes.

Serve with assorted crackers.

1 (14-ounce) can artichoke hearts, drained and chopped

1 (8-ounce) can crabmeat

1 cup grated Parmesan cheese

1 cup mayonnaise

¼ teaspoon lemon pepper seasoning

2 cloves garlic, mashed

salads

WHETHER YOU'RE SERVING YOUR DINNER BUFFET STYLE OR AS A FORMAL SIT-DOWN MEAL, A SALAD WILL ADD EYE-POPPING COLOR, FLAVOR, AND TEXTURE TO EACH PLATE. WITH TODAY'S CONVENIENT LETTUCES IN A BAG, YOU CAN ADD A FEW CUSTOM TOUCHES TO CREATE A SALAD THAT LOOKS AS THOUGH YOU'VE SPENT HOURS SLICING AND DICING.

THE FOLLOWING SALADS ARE TOSSED WITH THEIR OWN VINAIGRETTES OR DRESSINGS. SO HIDE THE BOTTLED DRESSINGS IN THE BACK OF THE FRIDGE AND EXPERIENCE THE WONDERFUL CONTRAST OF FLAVORS WHEN THE TASTE OF EACH VEGETABLE ISN'T MASKED BY A HEAVY DRESSING. THE KEY TO PREPARING A GREAT SALAD IS TO AVOID DROWNING THE LETTUCE IN DRESSING: USE JUST ENOUGH TO COAT EVERY DELICATE LEAF.

GOT A CROWD COMING FOR DINNER? SIMPLY MULTIPLY THE INGREDIENTS ACCORDINGLY.

Retro Salad Wedge (page 88).

almond-orange salad

Serves 4

DRESS UP YOUR CHOICE OF MIXED SALAD GREENS WITH A COMBINATION OF COLOR, TASTE, AND TEXTURE. VARY THE LOOK AND FLAVOR OF SALAD BY USING DIFFERENT TYPES OF GREENS, SUCH AS BOSTON, ROMAINE, ENDIVE, RADICCHIO, SPINACH, AND ESCAROLE—OR BUY PACKAGED SALAD GREENS AND THEN ADD YOUR OWN CHOICES TO THE MIXTURE.

Place the salad ingredients in a bowl.

Combine the hot pepper sauce, sugar, salt, pepper, vinegar, and oil in a food processor. Whirl until well blended and frothy. Refrigerate until ready to use.

When ready to serve, shake the vinaigrette, pour over the salad ingredients, and toss to coat.

SALAD

1 (16-ounce) bag mixed salad greens

1 cup thinly sliced celery

1 tablespoon minced parsley

2 green onions, sliced

1 (6-ounce) can mandarin orange slices, drained

¼ cup slivered almonds, toasted

VINAIGRETTE

¼ teaspoon hot pepper sauce

1 to 2 tablespoons sugar (to taste)

½ teaspoon salt (or to taste)

½ teaspoon pepper (or to taste)

2 tablespoons tarragon vinegar

¼ cup olive oil

salad greens with cranberries in port wine

Serves 4

$\mathcal{L}$OOKING FOR A COLORFUL AND FLAVORFUL WAY TO SLIP CRANBERRIES INTO YOUR DINNER MENU? THIS DELICIOUS SALAD IS FRESHLY DRESSED WITH AN UNPARALLELED MELDING OF TASTES. THE PORT WINE SWEETENS THE TART CRANBERRIES, WHILE THE CRUNCH OF TOASTED ALMONDS AND THE SHARPNESS OF BLUE CHEESE RESULT IN AN EXCEPTIONAL BLEND OF TEXTURES AND FLAVORS.

Soak the cranberries in the port wine overnight.

To make the dressing, place the oil, water, vinegar, hot pepper sauce, sugar, cinnamon, and salt and pepper in a food processor and whirl until emulsified. Pour into a container, cover, and refrigerate overnight.

When ready to serve, place the blended lettuces in a large salad bowl. Shake the dressing, then pour over the lettuce and toss.

Drain the cranberries. Garnish the salad with the cranberries, cheese, and almonds. Toss lightly.

½ cup dried cranberries

½ cup port wine

½ cup olive oil

¼ cup water

¼ cup raspberry vinegar

5 dashes of hot pepper sauce

1 teaspoon sugar

1 teaspoon cinnamon

Salt and pepper to taste

1 (16-ounce) bag blended lettuces (romaine, radicchio, butter lettuce)

¼ cup crumbled blue cheese

¼ cup sliced almonds, toasted

all-american chopped salad

Serves 4

STRAIGHTFORWARD AND UNASSUMING ICEBERG LETTUCE GETS A MAKEOVER WITH THIS PALATE-PLEASING BLEND OF FLAVORS.

To make the Raspberry-Dijon Vinaigrette, blend the mustard, raspberry vinegar, balsamic vinegar, olive oil, and pepper in a food processor until frothy. (The vinaigrette may be stored in the refrigerator for up to 2 weeks.)

To prepare the salad, heat the vegetable oil in a skillet. Add the prosciutto and cook, turning once, until crisp (about 5 minutes). Drain on a paper towel and crumble when cool.

Place the lettuce, avocado, onion, and tomato in a salad bowl and toss with the vinaigrette (remember, a little goes a long way). Sprinkle with the prosciutto and the cheese.

Note: The prosciutto or bacon may be prepared in advance and refrigerated until ready to use.

SALAD

2 tablespoons vegetable oil

4 slices prosciutto or bacon

1 head iceberg lettuce, chopped

2 avocados, peeled and diced

2 green onions, cut into ¼-inch slices

1 large tomato, cut into wedges

1 cup crumbled blue cheese (or a cheese of your choice)

1 cup Raspberry-Dijon Vinaigrette (or your favorite Italian dressing)

RASPBERRY-DIJON VINAIGRETTE

1 teaspoon Dijon mustard

¼ cup raspberry vinegar

2 tablespoons balsamic vinegar

¾ cup virgin olive oil

¼ teaspoon black pepper

all-american potato salad

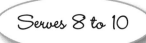

Serves 8 to 10

THERE SEEM TO BE AS MANY VARIATIONS OF POTATO SALAD AS THERE ARE PEOPLE, BUT THIS PARTICULAR RECIPE IS A REAL CROWD PLEASER. IT'S EASY TO THROW IN A FEW MORE POTATOES OR EVEN TO DOUBLE THE RECIPE IF NEED BE, AS LONG AS YOU KEEP A ONE-TO-ONE RATIO OF POTATO TO HARD-BOILED EGG AND ADJUST YOUR SEASONINGS ACCORDINGLY. USE MORE OR LESS OF EACH INGREDIENT TO SUIT YOUR TASTE.

THIS DISH IS BEST MADE A DAY IN ADVANCE, TO ALLOW THE FLAVORS TO BLEND FULLY. REFRIGERATE UNTIL READY TO SERVE.

Boil the potatoes until fork tender. Drain and cool, then slice and place in a large bowl. Gently mix in the eggs, onion, celery, bell pepper, and dill pickle.

In a separate bowl, combine the mayonnaise, mustard, and vinegar until smooth. Pour this over the over potato mixture. Season with salt and pepper. Stir carefully until thoroughly incorporated.

Refrigerate for at least 4 hours.

8 red potatoes, skins scrubbed

8 hard-boiled eggs, peeled and sliced

¼ cup finely chopped onion

2 stalks celery, chopped

1 red bell pepper, chopped

½ cup chopped dill pickle

¾ cup mayonnaise

2 tablespoons yellow mustard

2 tablespoons vinegar

Salt and pepper

retro salad wedge

Serves 6

THIS PRESENTATION OF ICEBERG LETTUCE WILL HAVE YOUR GUESTS MARVELING AT YOUR EXPERTISE. IF YOU'RE A DINNER GUEST AND HAVE BEEN ASKED TO BRING SALAD, THIS IS A GOOD CHOICE AS IT TRAVELS EXTREMELY WELL. IT'S MADE IN ADVANCE SO THAT THE FLAVORS WILL BLEND, ALLOWING YOU TIME TO ATTEND TO OTHER LAST-MINUTE DETAILS OR TO CHAT WITH THE OTHER GUESTS.

Hollow out the center of the lettuce, making sure that the outer shell of the head is approximately 1 inch thick (see below).

Beat the cream cheese, blue cheese, and mayonnaise until smooth. Beat in the bell pepper, onion, walnuts, chives, Worcestershire sauce, and hot pepper sauce.

Pack the mixture into the hollowed-out head of lettuce. Wrap the entire head in wet paper towels and then foil. Refrigerate for at least 2 hours. Cut into wedges and serve.

1 compact head iceberg lettuce

6 ounces cream cheese

⅓ cup crumbled blue cheese

¼ cup mayonnaise

2 tablespoons minced green bell pepper

2 tablespoons minced red onion

2 tablespoons chopped walnuts

2 tablespoons chopped chives

1 teaspoon Worcestershire sauce

Dash of hot pepper sauce

How to hollow out a head of iceberg lettuce

After washing the head of lettuce, hold it with the hard stem facing down. Hit the stem sharply on the counter once or twice. The core will be dislodged and, with a few wiggles and twists, easily removed. Continue to hollow out the core until the outer shell of lettuce is approximately 1 inch thick and the cavity is large enough to hold the filling.

seven-layer salad

Serves 6 to 8

THIS CLASSIC SALAD IS SO GOOD IT JUST REFUSES TO GO AWAY. FEW SALADS CAN BE MADE IN ADVANCE, BUT THIS ONE MUST BE MADE AHEAD, TO GIVE THE FLAVORS TIME TO BLEND. IT'S WONDERFULLY CONVENIENT TO TRANSPORT IF YOUR DESTINATION IS AWAY FROM HOME AND YOU'VE BEEN ASKED TO BRING THE SALAD. IF DINNER IS AT YOUR HOME, MAKE THE SALAD THE NIGHT BEFORE AND THEN RELAX WITH YOUR GUESTS.

Place the lettuce in the bottom of a shallow dish approximately 9 by 13 inches. Add a layer each of bell pepper, celery, onion, peas, and bacon.

In a separate bowl, mix the mayonnaise and sugar. Spread evenly over the bacon and vegetables to completely seal them in the dish. Sprinkle the cheese on top. Cover and refrigerate for at least 2 hours, preferably overnight.

1 head iceberg lettuce, torn into small pieces

½ cup chopped green bell pepper

½ cup chopped celery

½ cup chopped red onion

1 cup frozen baby peas

9 slices bacon, fried and crumbled

2 cups mayonnaise

2 tablespoons sugar

1 cup grated cheddar cheese

spinach salad with strawberries

Serves 8

Team your salad greens with a contrast of color for eye-popping presentation and taste.

Arrange the spinach, strawberries, and as many slices of onion as desired in a large salad bowl.

To make the dressing, place the sugar, sesame seeds, poppy seeds, minced onion, Worcestershire sauce, and paprika in a food processor. With the motor running, slowly add the oil and vinegar until thoroughly mixed and slightly thickened or frothy.

Pour the dressing over the salad and toss to coat.

Variations

- Substitute blueberries or raspberries for the strawberries.
- Add blue cheese or a cheese of your choice.
- Add toasted pecans or walnuts.
- Omit the red onion.
- Customize the dish to create your own signature salad!

SALAD

2 bunches fresh spinach and/or lettuce

2 pints fresh strawberries, hulled and sliced

1 small red onion, sliced

DRESSING

1 to 2 tablespoons sugar (to taste)

2 tablespoons sesame seeds

1 tablespoon poppy seeds

1½ teaspoons minced onion

¼ teaspoon Worcestershire sauce

¼ teaspoon paprika

½ cup vegetable oil or olive oil

¼ cup vinegar

sweet and crunchy coleslaw

Serves 8

CRISPY COLESLAW IS SCRUMPTIOUS WHEN SERVED IN THE MIDST OF A TANGY/SWEET BLEND OF FLAVOR AND CRUNCH WITH AN ASIAN TWIST.

To make the dressing, combine the oil, vinegar, sugar, and salt and pepper to taste. Mix well.

In a large bowl, combine the cabbage, onion, almonds, sesame seeds, bacon, and carrot (if using).

Pour the dressing over the salad and refrigerate for 2 to 4 hours. Just before serving, toss with the noodles.

SALAD

½ head cabbage, shredded, or 1 (1-pound) package shredded coleslaw

1 bunch green onions, thinly sliced

½ cup slivered almonds, toasted

¼ cup sesame seeds, toasted

5 strips bacon, fried and crumbled

3 carrots, shredded (optional)

1 (3-ounce) package chicken-flavored Ramen noodles, broken into pieces (omit seasoning mix)

DRESSING

½ cup oil

¼ cup cider vinegar

1 tablespoon sugar (or to taste)

Salt and pepper

cranberry and fruit side dishes

*C*RANBERRIES ARE THE QUINTESSENTIAL ACCOMPANIMENT TO THE THANKSGIVING OR CHRISTMAS FEAST, WHILE FRESH FRUIT ADDS COLOR AND ZEST TO YOUR MENU ANY TIME OF YEAR.

Cranberry Sauce (page 93).

cranberry sauce

Makes about 4 cups

THIS SIMPLE RECIPE HAS A GLORIOUS HISTORY. A WONDERFUL FRIEND OF MINE SHARED ITS RICH HERITAGE WITH ME. THE RECIPE ORIGINALLY APPEARED IN *WHITE HOUSE COOKBOOK*, PUBLISHED IN 1894. THIS BOOK, A COMPILATION OF RECIPES FROM THE WHITE HOUSE CHEF, WAS A WEDDING GIFT TO MY FRIEND'S GRANDMOTHER, WHO WAS MARRIED ON CHRISTMAS DAY 1907. HER GRANDMOTHER PASSED THE TRADITIONAL RECIPE DOWN TO HER DAUGHTER, WHO IN TURN PASSED IT ON TO HER DAUGHTER. EVERY YEAR SINCE 1907 THE DISH HAS GRACED THE FAMILY'S THANKSGIVING TABLE. NOW MY FRIEND HAS PASSED THE RECIPE ON TO HER OWN DAUGHTER.

1 quart fresh cranberries

2 cups water

2 cups sugar

Rinse the cranberries and place them in a saucepan. Add the water, cover, and simmer until each cranberry bursts open. Add the sugar and boil, uncovered, for 20 minutes. The cranberries must not be stirred (ever!) from the time they are placed on the stove until they are done.

Remove from heat, turn into a bowl, and refrigerate.

This sauce may be prepared a day ahead.

cranberry salad

Serves 8 to 10

A FRIEND OF MINE, A GREAT COOK FROM LOUISIANA, WAS GIVEN THIS CRANBERRY RECIPE BY HER GRANDMOTHER AND IS REQUIRED TO BRING THE DISH TO EVERY THANKSGIVING DINNER ON BOTH SIDES OF HER FAMILY. EVERYONE BELIEVES IT IS A TRADITION WELL WORTH PRESERVING. THE SALAD IS PARTICULARLY DELECTABLE WHEN SERVED IN AN ELEGANT CRYSTAL BOWL.

Drain the pineapple, reserving the syrup. Add enough water to the syrup to make ¾ cup. Set aside.

Combine the sugar and the gelatin. Dissolve in the hot water. Add the reserved pineapple syrup/water mixture. Refrigerate until partially set. Add the cranberries, celery, orange, and walnuts. Refrigerate until completely set.

1 cup crushed pineapple

1 cup sugar

1 (6-ounce) package cherry gelatin

2 cups hot water

1 cup ground fresh cranberries

1 cup chopped celery

1 navel orange with peel, finely choppd and seeded

½ cup chopped walnuts or pecans

cranberry-orange salsa

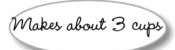

Makes about 3 cups

THIS IS AN ABBREVIATED VERSION OF CRANBERRY SALAD (PAGE 94). BY OMITTING ALL BUT THREE INGREDIENTS, ALTERING THE QUANTITIES, AND ADDING A JALAPEÑO, YOU'VE CREATED A SASSY SIDE DISH. THIS RECIPE IS A GREAT WAY TO ENHANCE THE FLAVOR OF TURKEY SANDWICHES. IT'S SURE TO WAKE UP YOUR TASTE BUDS!

In a food processor, chop the cranberries, orange, and half of the jalapeño. Pulse until chopped into small chunks. Transfer to a serving bowl. Taste for hotness and add more of the jalapeño if desired. Mix in the sugar.

Cover and refrigerate for at least 4 hours.

Note: This dish may be prepared up to 2 days in advance.

1 pound cranberries (fresh or frozen)

2 navel oranges, peeled, seeded, and cut into chunks

1 medium-sized fresh jalapeño, seeded and chopped

1 cup sugar (or to taste)

cranberry-port wine salad

Serves 8 to 10

So ELEGANT YET SO SIMPLE. THIS DELICIOUS CRANBERRY DISH IS ALSO CONVENIENT, AS IT STARTS WITH CANNED CRANBERRY SAUCE. YOU JUST GIVE IT A PERSONAL TWIST AND A LITTLE ZIP. THE PORT WINE CUTS THE TARTNESS OF THE CRANBERRIES WHILE THE CREAM CHEESE TOPPING MELLOWS EACH MOUTH-WATERING BITE.

To make the topping, thoroughly mix the sour cream and the cream cheese.

To prepare the salad, first dissolve the gelatin in hot water. Chill until firm but not set. Stir in the pineapple, cranberry sauce, port wine, and walnuts. Mix well. Transfer to a serving bowl and refrigerate until set.

The topping may be either placed directly on top of the salad or served on the side as a garnish.

SALAD

2 (3-ounce) packages raspberry gelatin

2 cups hot water

1 (8-ounce) can crushed pineapple

1 (16-ounce) can whole-berry cranberry sauce

¾ cup port wine

½ cup chopped walnuts or pecans

TOPPING

1 cup sour cream

3 ounces cream cheese

fresh fruit salad with glaze

Serves 8

In a small bowl, combine the cream cheese, sugar, and orange juice until well blended. Set aside.

In a large bowl, combine the strawberries, raspberries, blueberries, peaches, bananas, grapes, and oranges.

Pour the glaze over the fruit and gently toss to coat.

Garnish with the mint leaves.

GLAZE (OPTIONAL)

1 (8-ounce) package cream cheese

2 tablespoons sugar

⅓ cup orange juice

SALAD

1 pint strawberries, hulled and sliced

1 pint raspberries

1 pint blueberries

2 or 3 ripe peaches, peeled, pitted, and sliced

2 bananas, sliced

3 cups green and/or red grapes

1 (11-ounce) can mandarin oranges, drained

Fresh mint leaves

melon wedges with sweet berry sauce

Serves 8

In a medium bowl, combine the strawberries, blueberries, raspberries, orange juice, and sugar. Mix well. Refrigerate for 60 to 90 minutes.

Peel the melon and cut it into wedges. To serve individually, spoon the chilled berry mixture over each wedge. To serve a crowd, arrange the wedges on a platter and place a small bowl of the berry mixture in the center for guests to help themselves.

1 cup sliced fresh strawberries

1 cup fresh blueberries

1 cup fresh raspberries

½ cup orange juice

¼ cup sugar

1 honeydew melon or cantaloupe, halved and seeded

baked apples

Serves 6

Preheat the oven to 350°F.

Pare a strip around the top of each apple and press the brown sugar into the cavity. Place in a baking dish and sprinkle with the cinnamon. Top each apple with a pat of butter.

Bake, uncovered, for 30 to 45 minutes or until tender.

Baste the apple with the pan juices before serving.

6 baking apples, cored

½ cup brown sugar

Cinnamon

Butter

vegetable dishes

ROASTED OR BAKED, BOILED OR GRILLED, DEEP FRIED OR CREAMED—
THERE SEEMS NO END TO THE WAYS IN WHICH VEGETABLES CAN
BE PREPARED. TOO OFTEN A TURKEY MEAL BECOMES A PLATE OF
MONOCHROMATIC BEIGE. VEGETABLES CAN BECOME FLAMBOYANT,
COLORFUL SIDE DISHES THAT ADD FLAIR, TEXTURE, AND FLAVOR TO THE
MENU.

I HAVE TAKEN CARE TO SELECT RECIPES THAT CAN HANDLE A CROWD
WITH MINIMAL SUPERVISION ON THE PART OF THE COOK. THE MORE
YOU CAN PREPARE OR ASSEMBLE IN ADVANCE, THE MORE YOU WILL BE
ABLE TO RELAX UNDER PRESSURE AND ENJOY THE FESTIVITIES.

Roasted Corn Salsa (page 117).

roasted vegetable mélange

Serves 12

IF YOU CAN'T DECIDE WHICH VEGETABLES TO SERVE, GO FOR THEM ALL! DOUBLE UP ON YOUR FAVORITES, OR OMIT THE ONES YOU'RE NOT FOND OF. YOU'LL CATER TO EVERYONE'S TASTE WITH THIS EASY RECIPE. AND IF YOU'RE SHORT ON OVEN SPACE, SIMPLY PUT THE VEGETABLES IN A DISPOSABLE FOIL PAN AND COOK THEM ON YOUR GAS GRILL. CHOOSE A VARIETY OF VEGETABLES, APPROXIMATELY 5 TO 7 POUNDS IN ALL.

Preheat the oven to 425°F.

Place the onions, zucchini, bell peppers, carrots, squash, and mushrooms in a large, shallow pan. Mix the oil with the vinegar, garlic, basil, and salt and pepper. Drizzle over the vegetables and mix thoroughly.

Roast, uncovered, for 1 hour, stirring occasionally. Sprinkle with the parsley and the Parmesan cheese (if using) and serve.

Here are some further possibilities to include in your mélange:

- 1 bunch asparagus (about 1 pound), tough ends removed

- 1 eggplant, sliced

- 4 red potatoes, cut into slices or wedges

- 8 ounces cherry tomatoes, halved, added for the last 20 minutes only

2 large onions, sliced or cut into ½-inch wedges

2 small zucchini, cut into thick slices

1 red bell pepper, cut into thick slices

1 yellow pepper, cut into thick slices

1 green bell pepper, cut into thick slices

8 ounces whole baby carrots

1 yellow squash, cut into thick slices

1 pound mushrooms, halved

¼ cup olive oil

2 tablespoons balsamic vinegar

4 garlic cloves, minced

1 teaspoon dried basil

Salt and pepper

3 to 4 tablespoons chopped fresh parsley

Parmesan cheese (optional)

grilled vegetable skewers

Serves 8

Score big with grilled seasonal vegetables that are skewered then quick-cooked to a sumptuous finish. You may even succeed in getting one of the men off the couch and away from the football game long enough to handle the outdoor cooking! An extra hand is always appreciated when you're trying to bring everything to its gastronomic climax.

Choose from among your favorite vegetables. Cut the vegetables into chunks and place them on wooden or metal skewers. Place "soft" vegetables like tomatoes and asparagus on the same skewer, as they take less time to grill than "hard" vegetables like onions and peppers.

Brush or spray the skewered vegetables with olive oil. Season as desired. Grill over a medium-hot fire for 3 to 5 minutes, turning to ensure that all sides are cooked.

Remove the vegetables from the skewers, place on a platter, and serve hot.

Note: To really make your day a breeze, prepare the skewers a day in advance.

Here are some vegetable suggestions:

- Onions
- Green, red, yellow, or orange bell peppers
- Cherry tomatoes
- Zucchini
- Squash
- Mushrooms
- Asparagus

mixed vegetable casserole

Serves 8

THIS IS AN EXCELLENT DISH TO MAKE AHEAD AND REFRIGERATE. IF CHILLED, IT WILL REQUIRE AN ADDITIONAL 15 MINUTES IN THE OVEN.

Grease a 2-quart casserole. Preheat the oven to 350°F.

Cook the frozen green beans, carrots, and peas according to the package directions.

In a bowl, combine the onion, bell pepper, cream, mayonnaise, and half of the Parmesan cheese. Add the cooked vegetables and toss lightly.

Turn the mixture into the prepared casserole. Sprinkle with the remaining Parmesan cheese and bake for 30 minutes or until browned.

2 (10-ounce) packages frozen green beans

1 (10-ounce) package frozen chopped carrots

1 (10-ounce) package frozen baby peas

1 medium onion, chopped

1 green bell pepper, chopped

1 cup heavy cream

1½ cups mayonnaise

1 cup grated Parmesan cheese

zucchini shells stuffed with mushrooms and cheese

Serves 8

ONE ZUCCHINI SHELL CONSTITUTES A SERVING, BUT PLAN ON MAKING MORE—THIS DISH IS DELICIOUS! THE PREPARATION IS TIME-CONSUMING BUT NOT COMPLEX, AND THE DISH CAN BE ASSEMBLED A DAY AHEAD.

Cut each zucchini in half lengthwise. Scoop out the flesh, leaving a shell a quarter of an inch thick. Set the halves aside. Chop the pulp and set aside.

Heat the oil and sauté the onion. Add the mushrooms and garlic. Cook, covered, until the mushrooms give up their juices. Add the zucchini pulp. Cook, stirring often, until the liquid evaporates. Add the cream cheese, egg, parsley, chilies, salt and pepper, and a third of the Parmesan cheese. Simmer, stirring often, for 4 minutes. Let cool.

Fill each zucchini half with equal parts of the mixture. Arrange in a baking dish. Store in the refrigerator, covered, until ready to use.

When ready to cook, preheat the oven to 350ºF. Sprinkle the remaining Parmesan cheese over the stuffed shells and bake for 10 to 15 minutes or until hot. Lightly brown the tops by placing the zucchini under the broiler for 1 minute. Serve hot.

4 small zucchini

¼ cup olive oil

½ cup chopped onion

½ cup finely diced fresh mushrooms

1 clove garlic, minced

3 ounces cream cheese

1 egg, beaten

¾ cup finely chopped parsley

1 tablespoon chopped chilies, or more (to taste)*

Salt and pepper

1 cup grated Parmesan cheese

Canned chilies are available in the Mexican-food section of groceries and supermarkets.

squash fritters

Makes about 24 fritters

Note that the prepared squash should sit for at least an hour before being used for batter.

The batter can be made a day ahead, then covered and refrigerated. It will be an "ugly duckling" sort of batter the next day but will produce delicious fritters nonetheless. If using refrigerated batter, be sure to drain it before frying.

In a large bowl, combine the squash, onion, and salt. Let sit for at least 1 hour.

Transfer the mixture to a large strainer and squeeze out as much liquid as possible.

Place the mixture back in the bowl and add the baking powder, sugar, eggs, and flour. If the mixture is not thick enough to hold together, add more flour.

Using the utmost caution, drop the mixture, by the heaping tablespoon, into the hot oil in a turkey fryer. The fritters will expand to about 3 inches in diameter as they cook.

Brown the fritters on both sides. Drain on paper towels and serve hot.

3 cups shredded raw squash

1 medium onion, finely chopped

1 teaspoon salt

1 teaspoon baking powder

1 teaspoon sugar

2 eggs, beaten

½ cup flour

Oil

Note: If preparing this dish to accompany your deep-fried turkey, simply make the fritters in the turkey fryer while the cooked turkey is resting and the oil is still hot. Exercise caution when using a turkey fryer filled with hot oil. Add and remove items carefully to avoid splashing or spilling hot oil over the edge. Keep children and pets away from the cooking area.

glazed acorn squash with cinnamon and brown sugar

Serves 8

ACORN SQUASH GLAZED WITH CINNAMON AND BROWN SUGAR IS AN AUTUMN VEGETABLE AT ITS SEASONAL BEST. THE FRAGRANCE, COLOR, AND FLAVOR EVOKE WARM FEELINGS TRUE TO THE FALL SEASON.

Preheat the oven to 325°F.

Place the 2 squash halves, cut side down, in a buttered baking dish. Add a quarter inch of boiling water and bake for 45 minutes.

Meanwhile, make the glaze. Melt the butter and stir in the brown sugar, cinnamon, and nutmeg until dissolved. Remove from heat and set aside.

Carefully remove the squash from the oven and pour off the water. Using a paper towel to protect your fingers, slice the squash into quarters and place it back in the dish. Brush the glaze over the squash and return the dish to the oven. Bake for another 15 minutes, basting occasionally.

2 medium acorn squash, halved and seeded

1 stick melted butter

½ cup firmly packed brown sugar

1 teaspoon cinnamon

Dash of nutmeg

Talk Turkey to Me

your mother's green bean casserole

Serves 6 to 8

My mother gave me this classic recipe that for many is a sentimental favorite throughout the year. The time-honored dish was created in 1955, in the test kitchens of Campbell's,® the soup people, but many Americans have passed the recipe down through the generations believing it to be their very own. You can argue about who really created this trusty casserole . . . or you can just ask for seconds and enjoy!

Preheat the oven to 350°F.

In a 1½-quart casserole, combine the soup, milk, green beans, pepper, and three-quarters of the onion rings. Bake for 20 minutes or until hot and bubbling. Top with the remainder of the onion rings and bake for another 5 minutes.

1 (10¾-ounce) can cream of mushroom soup

⅔ cup milk

2 (9-ounce) packages frozen green beans, cooked

1 (2.3-ounce) can French-fried onion rings

¼ teaspoon pepper (or to taste)

green beans with bacon and blue cheese

Serves 4

IF YOUR MOTHER'S GREEN BEAN CASSEROLE (PAGE 107) IS TOO RETRO FOR YOU, FAST FORWARD TO THE PRESENT WITH THIS TRENDY, UP-TO-DATE DISH.

Cook the green beans according to the package directions. Drain.

In a skillet, cook the bacon until crisp, then remove. Drain the fat, reserving 2 tablespoons. Sauté the onion in the bacon fat. Add the vinegar and simmer, stirring well.

Turn the green beans into a casserole. Place the onion mixture over the beans and toss thoroughly to coat. Crumble the bacon and blue cheese on top of the green beans. Broil for 1 minute or until the cheese starts to bubble.

1 (9-ounce) package frozen green beans

6 slices bacon

½ cup chopped onion

1 to 2 tablespoons tarragon vinegar

¼ cup blue cheese, or more (to taste)

Salt and pepper

spinach and artichoke bake

Serves 6 to 8

THIS IS NOT THE TIME TO COUNT CALORIES . . . WE'LL DO THAT TOMORROW. THIS YUMMY DISH IS LACED WITH BUTTER AND CREAM CHEESE. WOW!

Preheat the oven to 350°F.

Cook the spinach according to the package directions. Drain.

Arrange the artichoke hearts in a greased 9 by 12-inch baking dish.

In a bowl, combine the spinach, melted butter, cheese, lemon juice, and cayenne.

Spread the spinach mixture over the artichoke hearts. Sprinkle with the breadcrumbs and dot with butter. Bake for 30 minutes.

2 (10-ounce) packages frozen chopped spinach

1 (16-ounce) can artichoke hearts, drained and chopped

½ cup melted butter

1 (8-ounce) package cream cheese, softened

1 tablespoon lemon juice

¼ teaspoon cayenne (optional)

½ cup breadcrumbs

1 tablespoon butter

spinach soufflé

Serves 6 to 8

It's a rags-to-riches story: take one lowly vegetable and turn it into a savory masterpiece. My friend's husband claims he hates spinach, but year after year he fills his plate with seconds of this soufflé. He says it doesn't taste like spinach. Even the kids forget they're eating spinach when it's part of this tantalizing blend of flavors.

Melt the butter in a saucepan. Whisk in the flour to make a roux. Gradually whisk in the milk, creating a velvety sauce free of lumps. Simmer for 3 to 5 minutes.

Preheat the oven to 350ºF. Butter a 2-quart soufflé dish or straight-sided casserole that allows room for expansion.

In a bowl, combine the spinach, mayonnaise, eggs, onion, Parmesan cheese, and salt and pepper. Add the sauce and mix thoroughly.

Turn the mixture into the prepared dish and bake for 45 minutes. Serve at once.

3 tablespoons butter

3 tablespoons flour

1 cup milk

2 (10-ounce) packages frozen chopped spinach, thawed and thoroughly squeezed

1 cup mayonnaise

6 eggs, well beaten

¼ cup minced onion

2 tablespoons grated Parmesan cheese

¼ teaspoon salt (or to taste)

¼ teaspoon pepper (or to taste)

broccoli casserole

Serves 8

ONE CHRISTMAS DAY I HAD THE HONOR OF BEING INVITED TO A FEAST AT THE HOME OF AN EXTRAORDINARY COOK, A MEMBER OF AN ITALIAN FAMILY WHO LOVE TO EAT AND WHO COOK TO CELEBRATE. THEY SERVE THIS CASSEROLE AT EVERY HOLIDAY DINNER THROUGHOUT THE YEAR.

Preheat the oven to 350ºF. Grease a 2-quart casserole.

Cook the broccoli just until heated through. Drain.

Mix together the mayonnaise, soup, onion, and eggs until well combined.

Place half of the broccoli in the prepared casserole. Cover with half of the mayonnaise mixture, then half of the cheese. Add another layer each of broccoli, mayonnaise mixture, and cheese.

Bake for 45 minutes.

2 (10-ounce) packages frozen chopped broccoli

1½ cups mayonnaise

1 (10-ounce) can cream of mushroom soup

1 medium onion, finely chopped

4 eggs, beaten

2 cups shredded cheddar cheese

brussels sprouts with browned butter

Serves 6

I GREW UP EATING BRUSSELS SPROUTS—"LITTLE CABBAGES," I CALLED THEM. MOM WOULD COOK THEM UNTIL THEY WERE FORK TENDER, THEN MASH THEM AND POUR BROWNED BUTTER GENEROUSLY ALL OVER. A LITTLE SALT, AND VOILÀ! THE SIMPLE THINGS IN LIFE ARE OFTEN THE BEST.

Bring the brussels sprouts to a boil and cook until fork tender and soft in the center (about 10 minutes). Drain.

In a separate pan, heat the butter until it foams and turns a delicate golden brown (3 to 5 minutes).

Pour the hot butter over the brussels sprouts and season with salt and pepper.

1½ pounds brussels sprouts, trimmed and halved

4 tablespoons butter

Salt and pepper

About browned butter

Browned butter adds a wonderful, rich flavor to cooked vegetables. Try it on green beans, broccoli, or cauliflower. You must use butter (not margarine), and it must be browned, not merely melted.

carrot gratin

Serves 8

Even those who claim to hate carrots love this gratin. It's a blend of mellow flavors with melted cheddar cheese and a crunchy crumb topping.

Cook the carrots until soft. Sauté the onion. Combine the onion with the soup and cheese and heat until the mixture is melted.

Preheat the oven to 350°F.

Place the carrots and the onion mixture in a buttered 1½-quart casserole. Mix well.

Melt the butter and blend it with the breadcrumbs. Sprinkle the crumb mixture over the top of the casserole. Bake for 45 minutes.

4 cups sliced carrots

1 medium onion, chopped

1 (10-ounce) can cream of celery soup

½ cup shredded cheddar cheese

1 stick butter

1½ cups prepared breadcrumbs

No prepared breadcrumbs on hand?

Improvise with a package of croutons. Place the croutons in a plastic bag and crush them with a rolling pin, or toss the croutons into the food processor for a whirl, and, voilà, you've got crumbs!

whipped sweet baby carrots

Serves 6 to 8

CARROTS AS YOU'VE NEVER HAD THEM BEFORE, WITH A LIGHT TEXTURE AND A MELLOW, SLIGHTLY SWEET TASTE.

Boil the carrots with the ¼ cup of sugar until soft. Drain and mash.

Add the butter, milk, and 2 tablespoons of sugar. Continue mashing and then whip until well blended.

2 pounds baby carrots

¼ cup plus 2 tablespoons sugar

4 tablespoons butter

3 tablespoons milk

grilled corn in husks

IF THE GRILL'S HOT, THERE'S NO BETTER WAY THAN THIS TO TASTE THE SWEETNESS OF CORN ON THE COB!

Add 1 tablespoon of salt to each gallon of water.

Soak the ears of corn in their husks for 30 minutes.

Remove the corn from the water and open the husks but do not remove. Discard the silk and brush the corn with the melted butter. Rewrap the husks around the corn.

Cook over medium-hot coals for 10 minutes, turning once or twice.

Fresh corn in husks, 1 or 2 ears per person

Cold water sufficient to cover corn

Salt

Melted butter or margarine

corn pudding

Serves 8

$\mathcal{M}$IDWESTERN CORN MEETS SOUTHWESTERN TASTE. A COMBINATION OF FLAVORS MAKES THIS A GOING-TO-THE-PARTY TASTE FOR HUMBLE CORN.

Preheat the oven to 350ºF. Grease a 1-quart casserole.

Sauté the bell pepper in the butter. Sprinkle the flour and sugar over the pepper to coat. Remove from heat.

In a bowl, beat the eggs. Add the pepper mixture, corn, pimentos, and salt. Mix well.

Turn into the prepared casserole and bake for 25 minutes.

Top with the cheese and bake until the cheese is melted and lightly browned (5 minutes).

1 medium bell pepper, chopped

1 tablespoon butter

3 tablespoons flour

1 tablespoon sugar

4 eggs, beaten

1 (10-ounce) can creamed corn

1 (10-ounce) can whole corn

1 (2-ounce) jar pimentos, drained and chopped

1 teaspoon salt

½ cup shredded cheddar cheese

roasted corn salsa

Makes about 2 cups

THIS PIQUANT RELISH, WHICH CAN BE MADE A DAY IN ADVANCE, IS A PERFECT COMPLEMENT TO ROASTED OR GRILLED TURKEY.

Preheat the oven to 450°F.

Place the corn, onion, poblanos, and bell pepper on an oiled baking sheet. Brush with the remaining oil. Bake until lightly browned (15 to 20 minutes).

Place the poblanos and bell pepper in a brown paper bag to cool (this will allow the skins to be easily removed). When the vegetables are cooled, husk the corn and chop the onion. Peel the poblanos and bell pepper, discarding any stems or seeds, and then chop the flesh.

Toss the vegetables in the marjoram and the salsa.

2 ears corn

1 medium onion, halved

2 poblanos

1 red bell pepper

2 tablespoons olive oil

1 teaspoon chopped fresh marjoram

½ cup green or red salsa

baked beans

Serves 12 to 15

No MATTER WHAT THE SEASON, TO SOME IT'S UNTHINKABLE TO HOLD A FAMILY GATHERING WITHOUT A POT OF DELICIOUS BARBEQUE BAKED BEANS. THIS DISH IS EASY TO ASSEMBLE AHEAD OF TIME—JUST REFRIGERATE AND BAKE.

Preheat the oven to 350°F.

Fry the bacon in a skillet until crisp. Discard the bacon, leaving just enough fat in the skillet to sauté the onion and garlic. Add the vinegar, mustard, and sugar.

Stir the onion and garlic mixture into the beans in a large bean pot or casserole.

Bake, covered, for 1 hour, then remove the cover and bake for 1 more hour (total cooking time: 2 hours).

Note: If the dish is made ahead and refrigerated, bake, covered, for 1½ hours, then remove the cover and bake for 1 hour (total cooking time: 2½ hours).

6 slices bacon, cut up

2 large onions, diced

3 garlic cloves, minced

¼ cup vinegar

1 teaspoon dry mustard

½ to ¾ cup brown sugar (to taste)

1 (28-ounce) can baked beans

1 (14-ounce) can butter beans

1 (14-ounce) can dark red kidney beans

1 (14-ounce) can black beans

cowboy beans

Serves 10

THIS DISH MAY BE MADE A DAY AHEAD AND STORED IN A CASSEROLE IN THE REFRIGERATOR. SIMPLY REHEAT IN A 350°F OVEN FOR 1 HOUR.

Fry the bacon in a skillet. Remove the bacon and set aside, reserving all of the fat. Sauté the onion and bell pepper in the fat.

Open the cans of beans and pour the liquid into the skillet. Add the mustard, sugar, and ketchup. Mix well. Simmer until thickened.

Crumble the bacon. Add the beans and bacon to the skillet and heat thoroughly.

1 pound bacon

1 large onion, chopped

1 large green bell pepper, chopped

2 (28-ounce) cans baked beans

¼ cup yellow mustard

½ cup brown sugar

½ cup ketchup

potato dishes

Another member of the supporting cast that deserves top billing on any menu marquee is the potato. Whether red, russet, Yukon Gold, white, or sweet, and whether mashed, baked, or au gratin, the potato simply must make an appearance at the table.

Cookbooks, magazines, and television cooking shows offer myriad potato recipes. Part of the fun of planning a holiday feast is flipping through magazines for a new recipe or digging out a family favorite from your recipe archives. If you're short on time, however, the following selections will get you wild reviews at the dinner table. Any critic would give each recipe a "two thumbs up"!

Smashed Potatoes (page 121).

smashed potatoes

Serves 6 to 8

YOU'LL ENJOY THE RICH FLAVOR OF POTATOES MASHED IN THEIR SKINS—PLUS THE CONVENIENCE OF NOT HAVING TO PEEL AWAY THOSE NUTRITIOUS SKINS. I PREFER THE UNIQUE TASTE OF RED POTATOES BUT YOU COULD OPT FOR WHITE OR YUKON GOLD.

Place the potatoes in a pot with enough water to cover. Boil until fork tender. Drain.

Add the Garlic-Herbed Cream Cheese and salt and mash until well blended. Slowly add as much of the milk as needed and whip vigorously with a spoon until fluffy.

2 pounds potatoes, skins scrubbed and cut into chunks

8 ounces Garlic-Herbed Cream Cheese (page 81) or a commercially prepared version

1 teaspoon salt

½ cup milk

make-ahead golden potatoes

Serves 8 to 10

THIS DISH TASTES LIKE MASHED POTATOES BUT CAN BE PREPARED WITHOUT ANY LAST-MINUTE FUSS. MAKE IT A DAY IN ADVANCE AND REFRIGERATE. AN HOUR BEFORE SERVING, SLIP THE PREPARED DISH INTO THE OVEN AND GET READY FOR COMPLIMENTS—THESE POTATOES ARE THE KISSIN' COUSINS OF MASHED POTATOES.

Boil the potatoes until fork tender. Drain, cool, and peel. Shred in a food processor.

Grease a 9 by 12-inch baking dish.

Melt half of the butter and the cheese together. Add the sour cream, onion, salt, and pepper. Combine this mixture with the shredded potatoes and mix well.

Turn into the prepared baking dish and, if making ahead, refrigerate.

Bake at 450°F for 45 minutes or, if chilled, 60 minutes.

Melt the remaining butter and drizzle it over the top of the potatoes just before serving.

3 pounds potatoes

1 stick butter

2 cups shredded cheddar cheese

2 cups sour cream

⅓ cup chopped green onion

1 teaspoon salt

½ teaspoon black pepper

creamy cheesy potato casserole

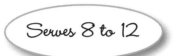

Serves 8 to 12

THIS EASY MAKE-AHEAD RECIPE USING FROZEN HASH BROWNS IS A GREAT TAKE-ALONG DISH IF POTATOES ARE YOUR CONTRIBUTION TO THE DINNER TABLE.

Empty the frozen hash browns into a large bowl. Thaw just enough to break apart.

Melt the butter and pour it over the potatoes. Stir in the soup, water, and sour cream. Mix thoroughly. Add the cheese and blend.

Turn into a lightly oiled 9 by 13-inch pan. Cover and refrigerate overnight.

Preheat the oven to 300°F.

Prepare the topping by crumbling the crackers and mixing them with the melted butter. Sprinkle the topping evenly over the potatoes. Bake, uncovered, for 45 minutes.

1 (32-ounce) package frozen hash-brown potatoes

1 stick butter or margarine

1 (10-ounce) can cream of chicken soup, plus ½ can water

12 ounces sour cream

16 ounces Monterey Jack cheese, shredded

TOPPING

50 buttery crackers

1 stick butter or margarine, melted

potato gratin

Serves 6

THIS DISH IS MORE SOPHISTICATED THAN THE TRADITIONAL FARE OF MASHED OR BAKED POTATOES.

Preheat the oven to 400°F. Grease a 9 by 13-inch baking dish.

Sauté the onion and garlic in 2 tablespoons of the oil. Add the bell pepper and continue to sauté. Remove from heat and add the red pepper flakes (if using) and 2 tablespoons of the basil. Set aside.

Spread half of the potato slices in the prepared baking dish. Sprinkle with half of the vegetable mixture and season with salt and pepper. Sprinkle with half of the cheese. Repeat the layers and drizzle with the remaining 1 tablespoon of oil.

Seal tightly with foil and bake for 30 minutes. Remove the foil and continue baking until the potatoes are tender and the top is golden brown (about 15 minutes). Sprinkle with the remaining 2 tablespoons of basil and serve.

1 medium onion, chopped

2 garlic cloves, chopped

3 tablespoons olive oil

1 red bell pepper, chopped

¼ teaspoon red pepper flakes (optional)

4 tablespoons chopped fresh basil or parsley

2 pounds baking potatoes, with or without skins, cut into slices

Salt and pepper

1 cup Gruyère cheese, shredded

roasted potatoes with
red onion and thyme

Serves 8

If you're seeking a combination of flavor and simplicity, look no further! These potatoes are roasted to a golden brown with an abundance of flavor. The dish is such a breeze to prepare you'll find yourself making it for regular weekday meals.

Preheat the oven to 350ºF.

Combine the potatoes, onion, and garlic in a 1-quart casserole. Sprinkle generously with the oil and season with the thyme and salt and pepper. Toss to coat evenly.

Roast until the potatoes are tender (about 1 hour).

2 pounds potatoes, halved and then quartered

1 large red onion, sliced

2 cloves garlic, chopped

¼ cup olive oil

2 teaspoons dried thyme

Salt and pepper

glorified sweet potatoes

Serves 8

Sweet potatoes are a time-honored tradition at the holidays. This colorful presentation transforms the lowly tuber into a glorious taste sensation. Even the pickiest eater will be back for seconds.

Grease a 2-quart casserole or a 9 by 13-inch baking dish.

In a large bowl, combine the sugar, milk, butter, eggs, vanilla extract, and sweet potato. Blend using an electric mixer set at medium speed.

Add the salt, cinnamon, and nutmeg and mix well. Add the pecans and raisins (if using).

Turn the mixture into the prepared casserole. If making in advance, cover and refrigerate until ready to bake.

Preheat the oven to 350°F and bake, uncovered, for 30 minutes, or, if chilled, for 45 minutes.

Place the marshmallows on top and continue baking until the marshmallows are lightly browned and partially melted.

1 cup sugar

1⅓ cups milk

1 cup melted butter

4 eggs, well beaten

1 teaspoon vanilla extract

4 cups sweet potatoes or yams, peeled, cooked, and mashed

½ teaspoon salt

½ teaspoon cinnamon

½ teaspoon nutmeg

1 (10-ounce) bag miniature marshmallows

½ cup chopped pecans (optional)

½ cup raisins (optional)

sweet potatoes with smoked cheddar cheese and cider

Serves 8 to 10

SMOKED CHEDDAR CHEESE AND CIDER BLEND TOGETHER TO PRODUCE A RICH, TANGY FLAVOR THAT IS SURE TO PLEASE.

Preheat the oven to 375ºF. Oil a 9 by 13-inch baking dish.

In a skillet, heat the remaining oil and sauté the onion. Remove from heat.

Assemble the gratin in the baking dish by using half of each ingredient. Start with half of the onion as a base layer, topped by half of the potatoes and half of the cheese. Season with the salt, pepper, and nutmeg. Repeat the layers but withhold the final layer of cheese until later in the cooking process. Pour the cider over the entire top layer. If desired, cover and refrigerate until ready to bake.

Bake, covered, until the potatoes are tender (about 45 minutes). Uncover and add the final layer of cheese, then continue baking until the cheese is melted.

4 tablespoons olive oil

2 large onions, thinly sliced

2 pounds sweet potatoes or yams, peeled and thinly sliced

½ pound smoked cheddar cheese, shredded (1 cup)

Salt and pepper

Nutmeg to taste

1½ cups apple cider

deep-fried sweet potatoes
with sugar and cinnamon

Serves 8

CRISPY DEEP-FRIED SWEET POTATO DUSTED WITH SUGAR AND CINNAMON! THIS IS ONE OF THOSE TASTY TREATS THAT COULD DISAPPEAR BEFORE IT EVER GETS TO THE TABLE.

SLICE THE SWEET POTATOES IN ADVANCE—THERE'S NO NEED TO STORE THEM IN WATER AS, UNLIKE WHITE POTATOES, RAW SWEET POTATOES DO NOT DISCOLOR. KEEP THE SLICES THIN.

Fry the sweet potato in hot oil in a turkey fryer. When golden brown (about 8 minutes), remove from the fryer. Drain on paper towels and dust with the sugar and cinnamon.

Note: If making this dish to accompany your deep-fried turkey, simply fry the sweet potatoes in the fryer while the cooked turkey is resting and the oil is still hot. Exercise caution when using a turkey fryer filled with hot oil. Add and remove items carefully to avoid splashing or spilling hot oil over the edge. Keep children and pets away from the cooking area.

5 pounds sweet potatoes, cut into ⅛-inch slices

½ cup sugar

2 teaspoons cinnamon

stuffing (or dressing)

Influenced heavily by regional distinctions, stuffing (or dressing), whatever its bread content, is as American as apple pie. From humble beginnings to its billing as a costar on the Thanksgiving menu, stuffing has a fairy tale past. In the story of Cinderella, the fairy godmother magically turns a lowly horse and some field mice into a glittering horse and carriage with coachmen. Likewise, stuffing starts from a modest foundation—day-old bread. Early Americans, letting nothing go to waste, created a dish that would grace our tables for centuries. With a little of this and some of that, the dried-out bread, like Cinderella and her escorts, is transformed with a bit of magic or, at the very least, cooking science. (In the absence of a fairy godmother, you can always use commercially prepared stuffing!)

"I'm from the South and we don't stuff our turkeys, honey, we dress them!"

The implication of the above declaration is that the Southern cook recoils at the thought of stuffing a turkey, preferring the genteel approach of serving the bread concoction as a side dish and calling it dressing. Purists use the term stuffing when the mixture is put in the bird and refer to it as dressing when it is served as a side dish. Indeed the terms are interchangeable, so whether your bird is stuffed or dressed, be sure to include one of the following recipes in your repertoire.

southern cornbread dressing

Serves 16

This recipe from a family with roots in Louisiana has been handed down, with some modifications, through five generations. Grandmother "Nannie" related the story of her own grandmother, Jane, who fell in love with an Irish immigrant. Jane had been widowed and was running a large farm when she met the handsome Irishman. They married but soon fell on hard times. They lost the farm and Jane lost her love. She was forced to move to the city and support herself. She was always known as a good cook, so when she managed to purchase a small inn it was only natural that, as an innkeeper, she would cook for her guests.

This recipe is intended as a side dish only; it is not to be used for stuffing the turkey.

Preheat the oven to 350°F. Grease two 9 by 13-inch baking pans.

In a large bowl, crumble the dried cornbread and combine it with all the other ingredients.

Divide the mixture evenly into the two prepared pans and bake, uncovered, for 1 hour.

Note: Uncooked dressing may be frozen for up to 1 month. Thaw completely in the refrigerator and bake, uncovered, for 1 hour and 15 minutes.

2 lots of Basic Cornbread (page 131) that have been left out to dry, or 2 (12-ounce) packages commercial cornbread cubes or crumbs

2 yellow onions, chopped

1 bunch of green onions, chopped

1 bell pepper, chopped

1 bunch celery, chopped

2 (10-ounce) cans cream of chicken soup

1 (10-ounce) can chicken broth

1 stick margarine, melted

6 to 8 eggs, beaten

basic cornbread

Serves 8

Grease a medium-sized (approximately 10-inch) iron skillet or baking pan and place it in a 350°F oven for 10 minutes.

In a bowl, combine the cornmeal, flour, baking powder, and powdered milk. Stir in the eggs and the oil and mix until the dry ingredients are moistened, adding water if necessary.

Carefully remove the skillet from the oven and place it on a protected surface. Turn the mixture into the skillet (it will sizzle as it comes into contact with the hot skillet). Bake until lightly browned (25 to 30 minutes).

VARIATIONS

Cornbread can be served as a bread side dish along with assorted rolls or muffins. You can tweak the recipe to evoke more of the flavors of the South by adding one of the following ingredients:

- ¾ cup cheddar or Monterey Jack cheese

- 1 (2-ounce) can green chilies, chopped

- ¼ cup finely chopped green onion

1 cup cornmeal

½ cup flour

3 teaspoons baking powder

½ cup powdered milk

2 eggs

2 tablespoons oil or bacon fat

Water (if needed)

old-fashioned bread stuffing

Makes enough for a 12-pound turkey

GIVE US THIS DAY OUR DAILY BREAD…AND WHEN WE'VE KEPT IT TOO LONG GIVE US STUFFING! SOME COOKS USE FRESH BREAD CUT INTO CUBES AND DRIED. MORE CREATIVE TYPES MAY FIGURE IT'S TIME TO CLEAN OUT THE BREADBOX AND USE ANY COMBINATION OF BREADS OR BUNS THEY HAVE ON HAND. THY WILL BE DONE…AS THE CREATOR OF THIS CULINARY MASTERPIECE, YOU CAN USE THE RECIPE TO STUFF OR NOT TO STUFF YOUR TURKEY.

Melt the 2 tablespoons of butter and sauté the onion and celery (about 5 minutes). Remove from heat and set aside.

Place the crumbled bread in a large bowl. Add the parsley, sage, marjoram, thyme, salt, pepper, and sautéed onion and celery. Toss to mix. Add the melted butter and blend well. Add the egg (if using) and thoroughly work into the stuffing mixture. Add the broth to lightly moisten.

If desired, loosely stuff the turkey, leaving a small mound of stuffing at the opening of the large cavity; this will become brown and crisp. If stuffing the smaller (neck) cavity, use the flap of skin to cover the stuffing and keep it secure.

- 2 tablespoons butter or margarine
- 1½ cups chopped onion
- 1½ cups chopped celery
- 1 loaf dried white bread, crumbled, or 1 (12-ounce) package commercial herbed stuffing cubes
- ½ cup chopped fresh parsley
- 1 teaspoon dried sage
- 1 to 2 teaspoons dried marjoram
- 1 teaspoon dried thyme
- ½ teaspoon salt
- ¼ teaspoon pepper
- 1 stick butter or margarine, melted
- 1 beaten egg or egg substitute* (optional)
- ⅓ cup to 1 cup chicken broth (as needed)

If you have any stuffing left over, or if you prefer to bake your stuffing outside of the turkey, place the remaining stuffing in a greased casserole. Add another sprinkling of broth: stuffing prepared outside of the turkey is dryer because it does not have the benefit of the turkey juices dripping into it. Cover and bake for 30 to 45 minutes depending on the amount of stuffing and the size of the dish. If you like your stuffing with a crust, remove the cover for the last 10 minutes of baking. Check the temperature with a meat thermometer. The stuffing temperature should be 160°F.

Cooks have traditionally used eggs in their stuffing. In today's world, though, the egg is often omitted in the interest of food safety. If you bake your stuffing to a temperature of 160°F, you should be safe in using an egg. If, however, you do not cook to the proper end temperature, you run the risk of salmonella. Egg substitutes pose no danger.

Do-it-yourself stuffing

Making your own stuffing is an opportunity to clean out the breadbox. The slices that remain at the bottom of the bread bag, day-old French bread, sourdough, or a slice or two of rye bread combine to produce stuffing with a depth of flavor. Removal of the crust is optional. To dry out the bread, leave it out of its wrapping in a single layer overnight. Alternatively, cut the bread into cubes, spread in a single layer on a baking sheet, and bake in a 400°F oven until golden brown (10 to 15 minutes), stirring occasionally; then allow to cool.

apple, sausage, and herb stuffing

Makes enough for a 15-pound turkey

Call it what you will—Yankee ingenuity, Southern hospitality, or Midwestern inspired—this collage of ingredients results in one impressive stuffing. The tart sweetness of apple complements the pork flavor.

In a skillet, crumble the sausage and cook until no longer pink. Remove to a paper towel so that the excess fat is absorbed. Drain the skillet, reserving 1 tablespoon of fat. Sauté the apple in the fat.

Place the prepared stuffing in a large bowl. Add the sausage and apple and mix well.

Use the stuffing either to stuff the turkey or as a baked side dish, being sure to first grease the casserole.

1 pound bulk Italian or pork sausage

1 pound Granny Smith apples, cored, peeled, and chopped

Old-Fashioned Bread Stuffing (page 132) or any commercial stuffing

rice stuffing with sausage

Serves 12

THERE ARE AS MANY WAYS TO MAKE RICE STUFFING AS THERE ARE TO MAKE BREAD STUFFING. SIMPLY CHOOSE YOUR FAVORITE RECIPE AND REPLACE THE BREAD WITH RICE. INSTEAD OF USING WHITE RICE, TRY WHOLE-GRAIN BROWN RICE FOR A NUTTIER FLAVOR AND MORE WHOLESOME GOODNESS.

Preheat the oven to 350°F.

In a skillet, crumble the sausage and fry until no longer pink. Remove and drain on paper towels. Reserve 2 tablespoons of the fat and sauté the onion, celery, and bell pepper. Remove from heat and blend in the parsley, sage, and salt and pepper.

Combine the sausage with the vegetable mixture and add the rice. Turn this mixture into a casserole and pour the broth over it, mixing well.

Bake, covered, for 45 minutes or until the rice is tender and the broth is absorbed. Fluff with a fork and serve.

1 pound bulk pork sausage

1 large onion, chopped

6 celery stalks, sliced

2 green bell peppers, chopped

3 tablespoons fresh parsley, chopped

1 teaspoon dried sage

Salt and pepper to taste

2 cups raw rice

3¾ cups chicken broth*

As a variation, replace 1 cup of the broth with 1 cup of white wine.

wild rice and mushroom bake

Serves 8 to 10

THE COMBINATION OF WILD RICE AND WHOLE-GRAIN BROWN RICE GIVES THIS STUFFING A NUTTY TEXTURE AND FLAVOR. IT IS LOADED WITH CELERY, SHIITAKE AND BUTTON MUSHROOMS, AND A VARIETY OF ONIONS FOR A HEARTY BLEND OF TASTES.

Preheat the oven to 375ºF. Grease a 2-quart casserole.

Sauté the onion, bell pepper, and celery in the butter. Sauté the mushrooms.

Mix the green onion, wild rice, brown rice, water, bouillon, and pepper together in the prepared casserole.

Bake, covered, for 1½ hours or until most of the water is absorbed. Drain off any excess water and serve.

1 large onion, chopped

1 green bell pepper, chopped

3 stalks celery, chopped

2 tablespoons butter or margarine

1 cup sliced shiitake mushrooms

1 cup sliced button mushrooms

2 green onions, sliced

1½ cups wild rice

½ cup whole-grain brown rice

3½ cups water, broth, or wine (or a combination of all three)

2 chicken bouillon cubes dissolved in ¼ cup water

Black pepper

new england oyster dressing

Serves 8 to 10

East coast, west coast, or anywhere in between, many Americans have a love affair with oysters—and oyster dressing is just one way to satisfy their desire. And if you restrict your oyster intake to months with an "R" in them, you're in luck. Thanksgiving falls in November, Christmas is celebrated in December, the Super Bowl is held in January, Mardi Gras usually takes place in February, and Easter falls in March or April.

Preheat the oven to 350°F. Grease a 2-quart casserole.

In a skillet, melt 1 tablespoon of the butter and sauté the onion and celery. Remove and set aside. Heat the remaining 2 tablespoons of butter until lightly browned and sauté the oysters.

In a bowl, combine the bread cubes with the onion and celery and the oysters. Add the oyster juice as needed to moisten the stuffing, but do not allow the dressing to become wet and soggy.

Place the dressing mixture in the prepared casserole and bake for 1 hour.

3 tablespoons butter (divided)

½ cup diced onion

½ cup diced celery

24 freshly shucked oysters, chopped, juice reserved

3 cups dried bread cubes

Salt and pepper

roasted chestnut stuffing

Serves 8

IF THE THOUGHT OF ROASTING YOUR OWN CHESTNUTS ON AN ALMOST-OPEN FIRE MAKES YOUR HEAD WHIRL, BY ALL MEANS USE COMMERCIAL VACUUM-PACKED CHESTNUTS INSTEAD.

First, roast the chestnuts. Preheat the oven to 400°F. Carve an X into the flat side of each chestnut and place the chestnuts flat side up on a baking sheet. Roast for 15 to 20 minutes or until the chestnuts are tender and their skins open up. Remove from the oven. When cool enough to handle, peel and chop.

Next, sauté the onion and celery in the butter. Add the mushrooms and continue sautéing.

Combine the chestnuts, thyme, marjoram, rosemary, broth, and salt and pepper. Mix well and adjust the seasoning and broth to taste.

Stuff the turkey, or place the stuffing in a greased casserole and bake at 350°F for 1 hour.

1½ cups chestnuts

1 loaf dried bread cut into cubes, or
1 (12-ounce) package herb stuffing mix

½ cup chopped onion

½ cup chopped celery

½ cup melted butter or margarine

½ cup chopped mushrooms

½ teaspoon dried thyme

½ teaspoon dried marjoram

½ teaspoon dried rosemary

½ cup broth (or as needed)

Salt and pepper

breads, rolls, and biscuits

A BASKET OF BREAD IS A FIXTURE ON ANY TABLE, AND IT CAN TAKE MANY FORMS, FROM CONVENIENT BROWN-AND-SERVE ROLLS TO FRESHLY BAKED COUNTRY BREAD. THE BREAD BASKET IS OFTEN AN AFTERTHOUGHT. SOME HOSTS TEND TO POP REFRIGERATOR BISCUITS INTO THE OVEN, OR BUY UNIFORMLY BROWN MASS-PRODUCED PUFFS OF BREAD, TOSS THEM INTO A BASKET, AND CONSIDER THE BREAD DETAIL COVERED.

WITH JUST A LITTLE FORETHOUGHT AND EFFORT, YOU CAN PREPARE MOUTH-WATERING HOMEMADE BISCUITS AND ROLLS. MAKE THEM AHEAD OF TIME AND FREEZE THEM. YOU'VE GONE TO THE TROUBLE OF PREPARING A FIRST-CLASS DINNER; PUT THE FINISHING TOUCH TO YOUR MEAL WITH THESE HOMEMADE DELIGHTS.

Sliced French Onion Bread (page 140) and
To-Die-For Cheese Biscuits (page 143).

french onion bread

Makes 2 loaves

𝒴OU DON'T HAVE TO BE AN EXPERT—YOU'LL JUST LOOK LIKE ONE!

In a large mixing bowl, combine 2 cups of the flour, the soup mix, the sugar, the salt, and the yeast. Stir well. Add the shortening and the water.

Using an electric mixer at medium speed, beat for 3 minutes. Gradually stir in the remaining flour, 1 cup at a time, to make a stiff dough.

On a lightly floured surface, knead the dough until smooth and elastic (about 3 minutes).

Place the dough in a well-oiled bowl and turn it around until the oil is visible on top. Cover with a damp cloth and place in a warm, draft-free, place until double in size (about 1 hour).

On a lightly floured surface, knead the dough a second time, punching it hard.

5 to 5½ cups all-purpose flour

1 envelope dry onion soup mix

3 tablespoons sugar

2 teaspoons salt

2 (.25-ounce) packages dry yeast

2 tablespoons shortening

2 cups hot tap water (120ºF)

1 egg white

1 tablespoon water

Divide the dough into two and roll out each half into a 5 by 14-inch rectangle. Fold it over lengthwise and use your fingers to pinch the side and ends closed.

Place the dough, seam side down, on a greased baking sheet. Cover and allow it to rise to double its size a second time (about 45 minutes).

Using a sharp knife, score the loaves by making 3 or 4 diagonal slits about half an inch deep.

In a small bowl, combine the egg white and the water. Brush this mixture over the loaves.

Bake at 375°F for 30 to 35 minutes or until the bread sounds hollow when tapped. Let it cool for 20 minutes before cutting.

Note: This bread can be frozen for up to 3 months. Let it thaw completely, then wrap in foil and heat in a 350°F oven for about 15 minutes.

pumpkin bread

Makes 2 loaves

A QUICK BREAD BURSTING WITH THE FRAGRANCE AND ESSENCE OF THE SEASON! PUMPKIN CAN BE USED IN MORE THAN PIES, AND THIS BREAD—ANOTHER FAMILY RECIPE HANDED DOWN THROUGH THE GENERATIONS—CROSSES THE LINE BETWEEN MAIN COURSE AND DESSERT. IF THERE'S ANY LEFT, USE IT FOR FRENCH TOAST THE NEXT MORNING.

Preheat the oven to 325ºF. Grease well two 9 by 5-inch loaf pans.

Beat the sugar with the oil until blended. Add the eggs one at a time, beating after each addition. Beat in the pumpkin.

In a separate bowl, sift the flour, salt, baking powder, baking soda, cloves, cinnamon, and nutmeg together.

Add the dry mixture to the pumpkin mixture and combine well.

Turn the batter into the prepared pans and bake for 1 hour. Cool in the pans for 10 minutes, then remove and finish cooling on a wire rack.

2 cups sugar

1 cup vegetable oil

3 eggs

2 cups canned unsweetened pumpkin

3 cups flour

½ teaspoon salt

½ teaspoon baking powder

1 teaspoon baking soda

1 teaspoon ground cloves

1 teaspoon cinnamon

1 teaspoon nutmeg

Talk Turkey to Me

to-die-for cheese biscuits

Makes about 24

THESE BISCUITS ARE RIDICULOUSLY EASY TO MAKE. JUST MIX, DROP, BAKE, THEN DRENCH IN DELECTABLE GARLIC BUTTER SAUCE. THE TENDER, BUTTERY MORSELS ARE SO GOOD YOUR GUESTS WILL THINK YOU STOLE THE RECIPE FROM THEIR FAVORITE RESTAURANT. YOU CAN EITHER SHARE THE RECIPE OR TELL THEM YOU CAN'T DIVULGE THE SECRET— IT'S PROPRIETARY INFORMATION!

First, make the biscuits. Preheat the oven to 400°F. In a large bowl, combine the biscuit and baking mix with the cheese, then add the water. Drop the dough by the heaping tablespoon onto a greased baking sheet and bake for 10 to 12 minutes.

Meanwhile, make the Garlic Butter Sauce. In a small bowl, combine the butter, parsley, and garlic.

Spread the Garlic Butter Sauce over the hot biscuits. At this point, the biscuits may be frozen if desired.

Note: Biscuits can be baked in advance and frozen. To reheat, simply place on a baking sheet and heat in a 400°F oven for 7 to 10 minutes.

3¾ cups all-purpose biscuit and baking mix

1 cup shredded cheddar cheese

1¼ cups water

GARLIC BUTTER SAUCE

6 tablespoons melted butter

1 teaspoon dried parsley

½ teaspoon garlic powder

lovin' rolls

Makes about 24

THESE ROLLS ARE EXQUISITE. IT'S NEARLY IMPOSSIBLE NOT TO CLOSE YOUR EYES AND SAVOR THE TASTE AS THE FLAVOR MELTS IN YOUR MOUTH. THE RECIPE WAS GIVEN TO ME BY A RENAISSANCE WOMAN WHO IS AS COMFORTABLE WITH A CIRCULAR SAW AS SHE IS WITH A FOOD PROCESSOR. IT CALLS FOR A TRULY HANDS-ON EXPERIENCE IN THE KITCHEN. THE DOUGH WILL TAKE SOME TIME TO RISE, SO GO AHEAD AND MULTITASK WHILE YOU WAIT FOR THE YEAST TO DO ITS WORK.

Mix together 3 cups of the flour, the sugar, the salt, and the yeast. Add the egg, shortening, and water. Mix. Continue adding the flour, 1 cup at a time. Combine well.

Place the dough on a lightly floured surface and knead it with your hands until smooth, soft, and elastic.

Place the dough in an oiled bowl. Turn it around and over until it is oiled on all sides. Cover the bowl with a damp towel or waxed paper and place it in a warm, draft-free place until the dough has doubled in size (about 1 hour). To determine whether the dough has risen sufficiently, poke it with your fingertip; if your finger leaves an impression, the dough is ready.

5 cups flour

½ cup sugar

1½ teaspoons salt

2 (.25-ounce) packages dry yeast

1 egg

¼ cup shortening, melted

2 cups hot tap water (120°F)

Place the dough on a lightly floured surface and knead it a second time. With your hands floured, punch it with your fists. Flatten the dough with your hands instead of a rolling pin, patting it down until it is half an inch thick.

Using a biscuit cutter or a round cookie cutter, cut the dough into circles. Place the circles on a baking sheet 1 to 2 inches apart (to allow for expansion). Cover the baking sheet with a damp cloth and let the circles rise until double in size.

Bake in a 350°F oven until browned (about 25 minutes).

Freeze and bake

Place the circles of dough on a baking sheet and put it in the freezer. When the circles are completely frozen, transfer them to a storage container and return them to the freezer. Remove from the freezer and use as needed; simply let the circles thaw and rise to double their size, then bake for about 25 minutes.

desserts

It's natural to feel a bit drowsy after a huge meal, so a nap may well be in order following dinner. But as the diners nod off in some cozy corner, truly believing they couldn't possibly eat another morsel, a heavenly aroma may begin to fill the air...

The beauty of the following desserts is that they can be made in advance. So put the coffee on, put your feet up, and enjoy the sweetness of life.

The Ultimate Cream Cake (page 164).

easy pecan pie

Each pie serves 8

NO ROLLING OUT OF PIE DOUGH, NO STUFFING OF TARTLETS—NOTHING BUT THE GOOD STUFF, TROUBLE-FREE AND FAST! IT ONLY LOOKS AS THOUGH YOU'VE SPENT HOURS IN THE KITCHEN.

First, make the crust. Blend the butter, cheese, and flour in a food processor until the dough forms a ball. Divide the dough and press into two pie pans.

Next, make the filling. Place the sugar, pecans, vanilla extract, eggs, and butter in a saucepan and heat, stirring, until hot (about 10 minutes). Do not boil. When the mixture starts to bubble, pour it into the 2 unbaked pie shells.

Bake at 350ºF until the crust is lightly browned and the filling is bubbling (20 minutes). Let cool for at least 45 minutes.

Dust with powdered sugar and top each serving with a dollop of whipped cream.

CRUST (MAKES 2 PIE SHELLS)

1 stick butter or margarine

1 (8-ounce) package cream cheese, softened

2 cups flour

FILLING (ENOUGH FOR 2 PIES)

2 cups brown sugar

2 cups chopped pecans

2 teaspoons vanilla extract

2 eggs

2 tablespoons butter

Powdered sugar

Whipped cream

southern pecan pie

Serves 8 to 10

THIS TRADITIONAL SOUTHERN TREAT IS BEST ENJOYED IN THE FALL AND WINTER WHEN PECANS ARE IN SEASON. SWEET, RICH, AND CRUNCHY, YET VERY EASY TO MAKE.

Preheat the oven to 350°F.

In a large bowl using a wire whisk, beat the eggs thoroughly with the sugar, corn syrup, margarine, and salt (if using). Add the pecans.

Turn into the unbaked pie shell. Arrange whole pecans around the top of the pie.

Bake until a knife inserted midway between the outer edge and the center of the filling comes out clean (50 to 55 minutes). The filling should be a little jiggly and the top lightly browned.

Allow to cool before serving. For added indulgence, serve with a dollop of fresh whipped cream.

Variation: Melt 2 (1-ounce) squares of unsweetened baking chocolate into the filling mixture before turning it into the pie shell. This will give a slightly richer flavor to the old standard. (No additional sugar is required.)

INGREDIENTS	9-INCH PIE	10-INCH PIE
Eggs	3	5
Sugar	⅔ cup	1 cup
Dark corn syrup	1 cup	1½ cups
Melted margarine	⅓ cup	½ cup
Salt (optional)	Pinch	Pinch
Pecan halves	1 cup	1½ cups
Whole pecans for garnish		
Unbaked pie shell		

pumpkin pie

Serves 8 to 10

$\mathcal{N}$OTHING SAYS TRADITION BETTER THAN PUMPKIN PIE.

Preheat the oven to 400°F.

In a large mixing bowl using a whisk, thoroughly combine the pumpkin, sugar, cinnamon, ginger, nutmeg, cloves, eggs, and milk. (The spices can be adjusted to taste.)

Turn the mixture into the unbaked pie shell. To avoid spilling, pull the center oven rack out to a convenient halfway position, place the pie shell on the rack, and pour in the filling (it will fill to a high level), then gently slide the rack back into the oven.

Bake until a knife inserted midway between the outer edge and the center of the filling comes out clean (50 to 55 minutes).

Cool before serving. Garnish with whipped cream if desired. For added indulgence, try a little honey drizzled on top.

INGREDIENTS	9-INCH PIE	10-INCH PIE
Canned unspiced pumpkin	1½ cups	2 cups
Sugar	¾ cup	1 cup
Cinnamon	1¼ teaspoons	1¾ teaspoons
Ground ginger	¾ teaspoon	1 teaspoon
Nutmeg	½ teaspoon	¾ teaspoon
Ground cloves	½ teaspoon	¾ teaspoon
Eggs	3	5
Milk	1¼ cups	1¾ cups
Evaporated milk	⅔ cup	1 cup
Unbaked pie shell		

apple crostata

Serves 4 to 6

A CROSTATA IS A FREE-FORM PIE—AND A STROKE OF LUCK FOR ANYONE INTIMIDATED BY THE ART OF PIE-MAKING. THIS RUSTIC TART IS EASY TO MAKE, WITHOUT THE FUSS OF CRIMPING A CRUST, AND WILL GAIN YOU RAVE REVIEWS WHETHER YOU ROLL OUT YOUR OWN DOUGH OR BUY A READY-MADE PIE SHELL.

Preheat the oven to 400° F.

Flour 2 sheets of parchment paper or aluminum foil. Place the dough on one of the sheets and cover it with the other. Roll the dough out into a circle 10 to 11 inches in diameter. Remove the top sheet and transfer the bottom sheet, with the rolled-out dough, to a baking sheet. (If using a refrigerated pie shell, place it on a sheet of parchment paper or aluminum foil and transfer it to a baking sheet.) Brush with the 1 tablespoon of melted butter and set aside.

Toss the apples with the flour, cinnamon, nutmeg (if using), and the 2 tablespoons of sugar to coat. Turn the mixture onto the center of the dough, leaving a border of 1 to 2 inches. Gently fold the border of dough over the apples and pleat it.

PASTRY

1 (9-inch) Basic Pie Crust (recipe on page 152) or 1 refrigerated ready-made pie shell

1 tablespoon melted butter

FILLING

2 large Golden Delicious or other baking apples, peeled, cored, and cut into ⅛-inch slices, then cut again into thirds

1 tablespoon flour

½ teaspoon cinnamon

⅛ teaspoon nutmeg (optional)

2 tablespoons sugar

1 tablespoon butter cut into small pieces

Milk

1 to 2 teaspoons sugar

1 tablespoon melted butter (optional)

Dot with the pieces of butter. Brush the dough with milk and sprinkle with the 1 to 2 teaspoons of sugar.

Place in the lower third of the oven and bake for 20 minutes. Reduce the heat to 350°F and bake for another 15 minutes. Serve hot.

For an added touch, brush the apples with the 1 tablespoon of melted butter and serve the crostata with cinnamon or vanilla ice cream.

basic pie crust

Makes 1 crust

A SIMPLE YET DELICIOUS CRUST THAT CAN BE USED FOR ANY PIE YOU MAKE. THESE INSTRUCTIONS CALL FOR THE USE OF A FOOD PROCESSOR, BUT YOU CAN ALSO DO IT THE OLD-FASHIONED WAY, USING A PASTRY CUTTER OR TWO FORKS.

Cut the butter into 6 pieces and place in the bowl of a food processor. Add the flour. Process, using the chopping blade on the pulse setting, until the mixture resembles coarse meal. With the motor running, slowly pour the water through the feed tube. Continue to process for 15 to 20 seconds or until the mixture forms a ball as it spins around. If more water is needed, add it in half-tablespoon increments. Avoid using too much water or the dough will be sticky.

Remove the dough from the bowl. Form it into a flattened ball and wrap it in waxed paper or plastic wrap. Refrigerate for 2 hours or overnight.

For easy clean-up, lightly moisten a clean cloth with water and use it to moisten a large area of countertop. Place a large piece of waxed paper over the moistened area (the moisture will make the paper stick securely to the surface).

INGREDIENTS	9-INCH PIE	10-INCH PIE
Cold unsalted butter	8 tablespoons	11 tablespoons
Flour	1 cup	1⅓ cups
Ice-cold water	2 tablespoons	3 tablespoons

Sprinkle flour on the waxed paper, on the rolling pin, and on your hands. Form the cold dough into a flat, round shape and place it on the waxed paper. Start rolling it out, rolling from the center to the edge in all directions. Lift the dough frequently to add more flour to the surface. Turn the dough over and continue the process. Keep rolling until the dough is round in shape and about an inch wider than the top edge of the pie pan. The dough should be about an eighth to a sixteenth of an inch thick.

Gently roll the dough over the rolling pin in order to lift it. Fit the dough into the pie pan, taking care to center it as much as possible. If it tears, make patches with pieces of dough using cold water as "glue."

Let the dough hang over the edges of the pie pan and then use a knife to remove the excess. For a decorative edge, cut strips of dough and lay them around the edge of the pie pan, using a dab of cold water to make them stick. Use a fork, tines dipped in flour, to press a pattern around the edge.

Fill the shell with your favorite pie filling and bake.

pumpkin roll

WHILE THIS CAKE ROLLED AROUND A CREAMY FILLING MAY REQUIRE MORE THAN AN OUNCE OF EFFORT, IT WILL BRING YOU POUNDS OF PRAISE.

First, make the cake. Preheat the oven to 375ºF. Grease a 10 by 15-inch jellyroll pan and line it with parchment or waxed paper.

In a large bowl, combine the eggs and the sugar. Beat well. Add the pumpkin and mix until well blended.

In a separate bowl, combine the flour, baking powder, cinnamon, ginger, nutmeg, and salt. Add to the egg mixture and mix well.

Spread the batter in the prepared pan and bake for 15 minutes.

Remove the cake from the pan and peel off the parchment paper. Let cool for 15 minutes. Place the cake on a clean dish towel or a sheet of aluminum foil and allow to cool for another 10 minutes.

From the side of the cake that measures 10 inches, begin to roll the cake, tightly and firmly, with the dish towel wrapped around it. Set aside.

CAKE

3 eggs

1 cup sugar

⅔ cup canned pumpkin

¾ cup all-purpose flour

1 teaspoon baking powder

2 teaspoons cinnamon

1 teaspoon ground ginger

½ teaspoon nutmeg

½ teaspoon salt

FILLING

1 (8-ounce) package cream cheese

4 tablespoons butter or margarine

1 cup powdered sugar

1 teaspoon vanilla extract

To prepare the filling, beat together the cream cheese and butter, then stir in the sugar and vanilla extract and blend until smooth.

Unroll the cake, remove the towel, and place the cake on a sheet of plastic wrap.

Spread the filling evenly over the inside of the unrolled cake. Roll the cake up and cover with plastic wrap. Slice off the ends so you have fresh end cuts and place the cake seam side down.

Refrigerate for at least 2 hours.

dark chocolate cake with decadent chocolate mousse frosting

Serves 10 to 12

THIS IS A MOIST CHOCOLATE CAKE WITH AN INCREDIBLY RICH AND CREAMY FROSTING THAT IS WELL WORTH THE EXTRA EFFORT.

Preheat the oven to 350°F. Grease and flour two 8-inch cake pans.

First prepare the cake. In a large bowl, sift together the flour, sugar, baking soda, and cocoa. Gradually add the mayonnaise, water, and vanilla and blend in. Turn the mixture into the prepared cake pans and bake for 30 minutes.

Meanwhile, make the frosting. In a sauce-pan, combine the milk and the flour to make a paste. Heat, stirring constantly, until thickened. It will have the consistency of library paste. Cool.

In a bowl, cream the butter and sugar. Add the cooled flour and milk mixture and the vanilla. Blend in. Add the chocolate and beat until firm but fluffy.

Cake

2 cups sifted cake flour

1 cup sugar

2 teaspoons baking soda

½ cup cocoa

1 cup mayonnaise (not reduced fat)

1 cup cold water

1 teaspoon vanilla

Frosting

¾ cup milk

5 tablespoons flour

1 stick unsalted butter

1 stick salted butter

¾ cup sugar

1 teaspoon vanilla

2 (1-ounce) squares unsweetened baking chocolate, melted and cooled

cranberry cake with warm butter sauce

Serves 4 to 6

†HIS QUICK DESSERT CAN EASILY BE MADE AHEAD OF TIME. IT'S AN OLD-FASHIONED BLEND OF GOODNESS THAT WARMS THE SOUL.

Preheat the oven to 375°F.

To make the cake, mix together all the ingredients. Turn into a square baking pan and bake for 30 minutes. Cool in the pan for 10 to 15 minutes, then remove from the pan and continue to cool on a wire rack.

Meanwhile, make the sauce. In a small saucepan, stir the butter, sugar, and milk together over low heat.

Pour the warm sauce over each serving of cranberry cake.

CRANBERRY CAKE

1 cup sugar

3 tablespoons melted butter

1 cup milk

2 cups flour

2 teaspoons baking soda

½ teaspoon salt

1 teaspoon vanilla extract

2 cups cranberries, each cut into 2 or 3 pieces

WARM BUTTER SAUCE

½ cup butter

¾ cup sugar

1 cup milk

grandma's down-home carrot cake

Serves 12 to 16

As a child my husband was very picky about food, with nary a vegetable coming near his little mouth. But one day his mother made a beautiful cake with frosting that just begged to have a young boy swipe his finger through it when no one was looking. Rumor had it, however, that this cake was made of carrots. A ghastly thought for a guy who lived on bologna sandwiches and moon pies®! Surely there couldn't be carrots in that cake. It looked too good, too delicious, like something one might actually eat. So he had a piece. He wouldn't believe his mother when she told him there were carrots in that cake. It sure didn't taste like carrots!

Today, carrot cake is my husband's favorite, and this is the recipe that he remembers from childhood. And today his mother tells her grandkids about the day when their finicky dad actually ate his vegetables.

Preheat the oven to 350°F. Grease and flour two 9-inch cake pans.

Beat the eggs. Beat in the carrots, sugar, and oil until well mixed. Add the flour, baking soda, vanilla extract, cinnamon, and salt and beat well.

Turn the batter into the prepared pans. Bake for 40 minutes or until a toothpick inserted in the center comes out clean. Remove from the oven. Let cool for 5 to 10 minutes, then remove from the pans and continue to cool on a wire rack.

Meanwhile, make the frosting. Blend the cream cheese with the powdered sugar and beat until fluffy. Add a small amount of milk if necessary to facilitate spreading, then continue to blend. Fold in the nuts and raisins (if using) and the coconut.

Spread the frosting between the layers and on the top and sides of the cake.

CAKE

4 eggs

3 cups grated carrot

2 cups sugar

1½ cups vegetable oil

2 cups sifted flour

2 teaspoons baking soda

1 teaspoon vanilla extract

1 teaspoon cinnamon

½ teaspoon salt

FROSTING

1 (8-ounce) package cream cheese

4 cups powdered sugar

Milk, as needed

1 cup chopped nuts (optional)

1 cup raisins (optional)

1⅓ cups coconut

raspberry-lemon marbled pound cake

Serves 6 to 8

THIS CREATION ONLY LOOKS AS THOUGH IT WAS HARD TO MAKE. MARBLEIZING TRANSFORMS A SIMPLE POUND CAKE INTO AN INTRIGUING INDULGENCE FIT FOR ANY SPECIAL OCCASION.

Preheat the oven to 325ºF. Grease a 9 by 5-inch loaf pan.

Combine the flour, salt, and baking soda. Set aside.

Beat the oil and sugar together at medium speed for 2 minutes. Set aside.

Stir the food coloring into the jam. Set aside

Combine the buttermilk, whole egg, egg whites, vanilla extract, butter flavoring, and lemon extract until well blended. Add the flour mixture and the oil/sugar mixture alternately, beginning and ending with the flour mixture. After each addition, beat at low speed until almost blended.

Divide the batter into three portions. Turn one portion into the prepared loaf pan.

Stir the jam into the second portion of batter, then gently spread it over the first

CAKE

3 cups all-purpose flour

½ teaspoon salt

½ teaspoon baking soda

1 cup vegetable oil

2½ cups sugar

10 drops red food coloring

¼ cup seedless raspberry jam

1 cup buttermilk

1 large egg

4 egg whites

1 teaspoon vanilla extract

1 teaspoon butter flavoring

1 teaspoon lemon extract

LEMON GLAZE (OPTIONAL)

1 cup powdered sugar

1 tablespoon lemon juice

1 tablespoon milk

portion. Spoon the third portion of batter on top of the jam portion. Using a spoon, gently scoop the bottom batter and bring it to the top to create a marble swirl effect. Repeat five or six times, being careful not to completely blend the batters.

Bake for 1 hour and 35 minutes or until a wooden toothpick inserted in the center comes out clean.

Cool in the pan on a wire rack for 10 to 15 minutes, then remove from the pan and allow to cool completely on the rack.

To prepare the optional Lemon Glaze, mix all the ingredients together until smooth (makes about 1 cup). Spoon the glaze over the warm cake if desired.

classic cheesecake

Serves 8 to 10

YOU CAN MAKE YOUR OWN GRAHAM-CRACKER CRUST OR USE A COMMERCIALLY PREPARED ONE. EITHER WAY, CHEESECAKE IS A TRADITIONAL DESSERT THAT HAS THE ABILITY TO CHANGE FLAVORS AS EASILY AS A CHAMELEON CHANGES COLORS. WE'LL BEGIN WITH THE CLASSIC VERSION AND THEN ADD A FEW OPTIONS FOR THE ADVENTURESOME.

THIS DESSERT IS BEST MADE A DAY IN ADVANCE, TO ALLOW THE FLAVORS TO BLEND.

Preheat the oven to 350°F.

First, make the crust. Crush the crackers in a food processor. Blend in the sugar, cinnamon (if using), and butter. Press the mixture into the bottom of a springform pan.

Next, make the filling. Beat the cream cheese at low speed. Gradually add the sugar. Add the eggs one at a time, beating well after each addition. Add the sour cream, lemon juice, heavy cream, and vanilla extract. Beat until creamy and smooth.

Turn the filling into the prepared pan and bake for 1 hour. Turn off the oven and leave the cheesecake in the oven for 1 more hour. Remove from the oven and refrigerate for at least several hours.

CRUST

12 graham crackers (1½ cups)

3 tablespoons brown sugar

1 teaspoon cinnamon (optional)

6 tablespoons melted butter

FILLING

3 (8-ounce) packages cream cheese

1½ cups sugar

4 eggs

2 cups sour cream

2 tablespoons plus ½ teaspoon lemon juice

1 cup heavy cream

½ teaspoon vanilla extract

CHERRY CHEESECAKE

Open a can of cherry pie filling and place the cherries in a beautiful glass bowl. When serving the cake, top each slice with a generous spoonful of cherries. Hide the empty can and serve!

PINEAPPLE CHEESECAKE

Add 1 cup of crushed pineapple (drained) to the cheesecake filling. Bake as directed.

PUMPKIN CHEESECAKE

Add ½ cup of canned pumpkin, ½ teaspoon of cinnamon, a dash of ground cloves, and a dash of nutmeg to the cheesecake filling. Mix well and bake as directed. When serving, garnish each slice with a dollop of whipped cream.

the ultimate cream cake

Serves 12 to 16

THIS IS A MAGNIFICENT BLEND OF FLAVORS AND TEXTURES THAT WILL QUICKLY BECOME THE DESSERT OF CHOICE AT YOUR HOLIDAY TABLE.

First, make the cake. Preheat the oven to 325ºF. Grease and flour three 9-inch cake pans.*

Combine the buttermilk and baking soda. Set aside.

In a separate bowl, cream the sugar with the butter and shortening. Add half of the buttermilk and baking soda mixture alternately with half of the flour and beat until smooth. Repeat with the remaining buttermilk and baking soda and the remaining flour. Stir in the vanilla extract. Set aside.

In a separate bowl, beat the egg whites until they stand in soft peaks. Gently fold this into the butter/sugar/flour mixture. Stir in the pecans and the coconut.

Bake for 25 minutes. Let rest for 5 to 10 minutes and then cool on a wire rack.

Meanwhile, prepare the frosting. Cream together the cream cheese and butter. Add the vanilla extract and blend. Beat

CAKE

1 cup buttermilk

1 tablespoon baking soda

2 cups sugar

1 stick butter or margarine

½ cup shortening

2 cups all-purpose flour, sifted

1 tablespoon vanilla extract

5 egg whites

1 cup chopped pecans

1 (4-ounce) can coconut

FROSTING

1 (8-ounce) package cream cheese

1 stick butter or margarine

1 teaspoon vanilla extract

4 cups powdered sugar

in the sugar in 1-cup quantities until fully incorporated.

When the three layers are cooled, frost each one and assemble the cake.

If you're short on time, this cake can be made in sheet form. Using a 9 by 13-inch greased and floured pan, bake for 30 to 35 minutes or until done. Let rest for 5 to 10 minutes, then cool on a wire rack. When completely cooled, frost the top and sides.

french silk pie

Serves 8 to 10

CHOCOLATE LOVERS WILL SCRAMBLE TO INDULGE IN THIS SINFULLY DELICIOUS PIE. RICH, SMOOTH, AND SO EASY TO MAKE, IT'S SURE TO BECOME A YEAR-ROUND FAVORITE IN YOUR HOUSEHOLD.

Cream the butter and slowly add the sugar. Beat in the chocolate. Add the vanilla extract and mix well. Add the eggs one at a time, beating thoroughly until well combined. Beat the mixture at high speed for 4 minutes.

Spoon the mixture into the baked pie shell and refrigerate. Before serving, garnish with chocolate shavings or whipped cream.

2 sticks unsalted butter, softened

2 cups powdered sugar

2 ounces (2 squares) unsweetened chocolate, melted and cooled

1 teaspoon vanilla extract

2 eggs (or egg substitute)

1 baked pie shell

Chocolate shavings or whipped cream for garnish

cappuccino cream pie

Serves 6 to 8

CLOUDS OF WHIPPED CREAM AND SWIRLS OF CREAM CHEESE ARE BLENDED WITH KAHLUA® AND COFFEE TO MAKE THIS CREAMY DREAM OF A DESSERT.

First, make the crust. Crush the chocolate wafers and combine them with the butter. Press the mixture into a 9-inch pie pan and freeze for at least 10 minutes.

Next, prepare the filling. Whip the cream until it stands in soft peaks.

In a separate bowl, beat the cream cheese with the sugar until blended.

Dissolve the coffee in a cup; add the Kahlua® and the cinnamon. Pour this into the cream cheese mixture and blend.

Fold the whipped cream into the cream cheese mixture, reserving a small amount for the top of the pie. Spoon the filling into the crust and spread a thin layer of the reserved whipped cream on top. Refrigerate until ready to serve.

CRUST

1 (9-ounce) package chocolate wafers (reserve 6 for garnish)

⅓ cup melted butter

FILLING

2 cups heavy cream

1 (8-ounce) package cream cheese

½ cup sugar

2 teaspoons instant coffee

3 tablespoons Kahlua®

1 teaspoon cinnamon

baked maple bananas

Serves 8 to 10

THIS HEAVENLY (AND QUICK) SIDE DISH IS EASILY TRANSFORMED INTO A DIVINE DESSERT WHEN PAIRED WITH VANILLA ICE CREAM.

Melt the butter in a microwave-safe baking dish. Add the syrup and combine. Add the bananas and turn gently until coated.

Microwave on high for 1 minute, stir, and then microwave on high for 1 more minute.

Stir in the lemon juice and sprinkle with the cinnamon. Serve warm.

½ cup butter

½ cup maple syrup

8 bananas, cut in half crosswise and then lengthwise

2 tablespoons lemon juice

¾ teaspoon cinnamon

strawberries and devonshire cream

Serves 8

In a small bowl, combine the cream cheese, sugar, and 4 tablespoons of the cream. Add one or two drops of the food coloring (if using). Beat until fluffy.

In a separate bowl, whip the remaining cream until it stands in soft peaks.

Fold the whipped cream into the cheese mixture. Turn into a serving bowl and place in the center of a platter. Surround the bowl with the strawberries.

1 (8-ounce) package cream cheese

4 tablespoons sugar

1 cup heavy cream

Red food coloring (optional)

Whole fresh strawberries, with stems

turkey straight talk:
everything you'll ever need to know

Common Terms and Equivalents

*E*veryone needs help from time to time with an equivalent measure or a cooking term. Whether you're on memory overload and don't want to remember one more thing, or you're new to cooking and haven't the slightest idea what's meant by "whisking," use this section as a guide. Use it, don't lose it!

Unit Measure Equivalents	
3 teaspoons	1 tablespoon
4 tablespoons	¼ cup
5⅓ tablespoons	⅓ cup
8 tablespoons	½ cup
10⅔ tablespoons	⅔ cup
12 tablespoons	¾ cup
16 tablespoons	1 cup
1 cup	½ pint
2 cups	1 pint
4 cups	1 quart
4 quarts	1 gallon

To measure accurately, use appropriate measuring utensils made of metal, plastic, or glass.

Dry ingredients are measured most accurately in individual cups calibrated by the unit of measure. These fractional sizes are sold as a set to allow for an exact measure for each fractional cup size. Lightly fill the measuring utensil and run the straight edge of a knife across the top. An exception to this rule is brown sugar. Brown sugar should be pressed into the fractional cup firmly so that when it is turned out of the cup it retains its shape—like wet sand at the beach.

A liquid measuring cup will be made of clear glass or plastic and have hash marks on its side denoting the unit of liquid to be measured. Measure the liquid on a level surface and bend down to read the mark—which would be at the bottom of the meniscus. By bending down to see the lowest point of the liquid in the measuring cup, you'll get a more accurate reading.

Measuring spoons are used for either dry or liquid ingredients. Always level off dry ingredients with a straight edge.

Jive Talk: Converting Your Measurements to Metric

It could be a hot issue if you happen to "swing the other way." While it may be a matter of great debate, your performance in the kitchen hinges on getting the measurements right. Regardless of your orientation, you may or may not be accustomed to deciphering the complicated formulas needed to convert a recipe from the customary unit of measure in America to the international standard unit of measure (using the metric system).

No complex mathematical formulas are needed here. This simple visual aid will help you to convert one measure into the other and will allow you to swing both ways!

TURKEY THAWING GUIDE		
Weight in pounds	Weight in kilograms	Refrigerator thawing time (days)
5 to 8	2 to 4	2
8 to 11	4 to 5	3
11 to 18	5 to 8	3 to 4
18 to 22	8 to 10	4 to 5
22 to 24	10 to 11	5 to 6
24 to 29	11 to 13	6 or more

DETERMINING DONENESS	
Stuffing	72°C
Breast	77°C
Thigh	83°C

DOES SIZE REALLY MATTER? TURKEY BUYING GUIDE	
Without leftovers	2.2 kilograms per person
With leftovers	3.3 kilograms per person

TEMPERATURE SETTINGS	
Fahrenheit	Celsius
160°	71°
170°	77°
180°	82°
200°	93°
250°	121°
300°	150°
325°	160°
350°	180°
400°	205°
450°	232°

CONVERSION GUIDE	
Volume	Milliliters (mL)
¼ teaspoon	1
½ teaspoon	2
1 teaspoon	5
1 tablespoon	15
¼ cup	60
⅓ cup	75
½ cup	125
¾ cup	180
1 cup	240

Terms of Endearment: The Language of Recipes

Bake – Cook using dry heat in an oven or similar appliance. When meat is cooked uncovered in an oven, it is referred to as roasting.

Baste – Moisten with drippings, butter, or another liquid during cooking.

Beat – Stir a mixture vigorously in order to blend the ingredients.

Boil – Bring a liquid to the boiling point of 212°F at sea level, producing bubbles that rise to the surface and burst. Water boils at a lower point at higher altitudes.

Broil – Cook using direct heat in an oven or broiler.

Chill – Place in the refrigerator to reduce the temperature.

Cream – Beat with an electric mixer until soft and smooth.

Cut in – Mix shortening with dry ingredients using a pastry blender or food processor.

Dice – Cut into small cubes.

Dissolve – Make a solution by mixing dry ingredients with a liquid.

Fold – Blend ingredients into a mixture gently by turning one part over the other.

Fry – Cook in hot oil or shortening over direct heat.

Glaze – Coat a food with a liquid substance that will set and become firm, smooth, and glossy.

Grate – Rub on an implement called a grater in order to produce small particles.

Knead – Work dough into a uniform mixture by pressing, folding, and stretching using the heels of your hands.

Marinate – Let food steep or bathe in a liquid to enhance flavor.

Mince – Cut into very fine pieces.

Mix – Combine ingredients by stirring until well blended.

Panfry – Cook uncovered in hot oil.

Pit – Remove the center pit from a fruit.

Roast – Cook meat uncovered in an oven and without water.

Roux – A cooked mixture of flour and butter or other fat used to thicken sauces and soups.

Sauté – Cook in a skillet with a small amount of butter or oil over a lively fire.

Scallop – Bake in a casserole with sauce, often topped with breadcrumbs or cheese (e.g., scalloped potatoes).

Score – Cut a notch or small slit in the surface of a food.

Shred – Rub food against a shredding surface to form long, narrow pieces.

Sift – Put a dry ingredient through a sifter or sieve.

Simmer – Cook over low heat so that bubbles break just below the surface at a slow rate.

Spritz – Spray briefly or quickly.

Steam – Cook in a covered pan using a small amount of water so that steam forms; water may or may not be added during the steaming process.

Stir – Mix ingredients, using a circular motion, until they are well blended.

Toss – Mix ingredients lightly but thoroughly.

Truss – Secure the legs or open cavity of poultry using skewers or string.

Whip – Rapidly beat a mixture in order to incorporate air and therefore expand the product.

Whisk – Blend a mixture, employing an implement called a whisk, using a rapid, circular motion.

Storing and Serving Leftovers

"I didn't know you could reheat poultry. I didn't know you could freeze it either."

Food companies have made tens of millions of dollars by freezing and reheating poultry in the form of TV dinners and the like!

The dinner is over and the guests are getting drowsy on the couch but the remains of the feast need to be put away. In the interests of food safety, it is essential that you refrigerate your leftover turkey within 2 hours of taking it out of the oven.

"We live in Canada and after dinner we put the turkey outside in a snow bank because the refrigerator was full. Last night we had another snowstorm roll in and it covered up our leftovers. We can't find them! I guess we'll have to dig around the yard a little."

〰

*W*hether your preference in storage containers is Tupperware® or Ziploc® bags, remove the stuffing from the turkey, cut the meat from the carcass, and pack it all up. These leftovers can be stored in the refrigerator for up to 3 days. For optimum flavor, frozen leftover turkey is best used within 3 months. If kept longer it may become dry and tasteless.

It appears that some people aren't fond of leftovers while others don't even know when they're eating them. Our kids cringe at the thought, our significant others state emphatically that they hate leftovers, and some of us just can't imagine making an edible meal from something that's "left over."

But when we go to the store to buy a frozen entrée, in reality we're buying a "leftover"—a prepared meal frozen at one time to be reheated and served at another time. The next time you drop by your local gourmet shop to pick up a tantalizing chicken salad, keep in mind that the dish originated as a roasted chicken. The bird was deboned, chopped, and mixed with vegetables and sauce, and voilà—a new beginning. Each time you reach into the cupboard for a can of soup, in fact, you're choosing to have a leftover. It's something that was prepared at one time and packaged to be opened and consumed at another time—a leftover.

Perhaps our aversion to leftovers has to do with the name we've given to them. The word leftover is bland and lackluster. But when we go to our favorite restaurant and order the Chef's Special—well, that sounds exciting, as though a lot of thought has gone into its preparation. It's the chef's special creation prepared exclusively for tonight!

So let's banish the word leftover and learn to think like a chef. It's not a leftover turkey sandwich but a Grilled Turkey Panini. You can present an encore of yesterday's feast but, with just a pixie dust of chef's imagination, transform the same food into a Creamed Turkey Potpie. So slice and chop that turkey into a Cobb Salad, or toss it with pasta and call it Turkey Tetrazzini. You're not serving leftovers. You're serving the Special of the Day!

A Page from the Little Black Book of Hot Numbers

The numbers included within the pages of the proverbial Little Black Book are usually top secret. The conquests below, however, gladly offer their numbers and even go out of their way to seduce you with their favors and wares. The first-generation 800 numbers are still there, but also included is a wealth of Web pages offering the consumer not only product and technical information but also a sensual world of colorful visuals, recipes, and kitchen tips.

Argo Cornstarch	866-373-2300	www.argostarch.com
Betty Crocker	800-446-1898	www.BettyCrocker.com
Butterball Turkey Talkline	800-288-8372	www.butterball.com
Campbell's Soup	800-257-8443	www.campbellskitchen.com
Clabber Girl Baking Powder		www.clabbergirl.com
Colorado State University Cooperative Extension		www.extcolostate.edu
Crisco	800-766-7309	www.crisco.com
Diamond Nuts		www.diamondnuts.com
Duncan Hines	800-362-9834	www.duncanhines.com
Fleishmann's Yeast	800-777-4959	www.breadworld.com
French's Onion Rings	800-841-1256	www.frenchsfoods.com
Ghirardelli Chocolate		www.ghirardelli.com
Green Giant	800-998-9996	www.greengiant.com
Jennie-O	800-621-3505	www.JennieOturkeystore.com
Keebler	877-453-5837	www.keebler.com
Kingsford Charcoal	800-232-4745	www.kingsford.com

Kraft Foods	800-634-1984	www.kraftfoods.com
Land O'Lakes	800-328-4155	www.landolakes.com
Libby's	800-854-0374	www.verybestbaking.com
LouAna Peanut Oil	800-723-3652	www.louanna.com
Mrs. Smith's Pies		www.mrs.smith.com
Nabisco	800-323-0768	www.nabiscoworld.com
National Turkey Federation	800-235-7206	www.eatturkey.com
Nestlé	800-289-7314	www.nestle.com
Ocean Spray Cranberries	800-662-3263	www.oceanspray.com
Pepperidge Farm	888-737-7374	www.pfgoldfish.com
Planters	877-677-3268	www.planters.com
Pillsbury	800-775-4777	www.pillsbury.com
Reynolds Kitchens	800-745-4000	www.reynoldskitchen.com
Sara Lee	800-323-7117	www.saraleebakery.com
Spice Islands	800-247-5251	www.spiceislands.com
Sun Maid Raisins		www.sunmaid.com
Swanson	800-442-7684	www.swansonbroth.com
Talk Turkey To Me		www.talkturkeytome.com
Uncle Ben's	800-548-6253	www.unclebens.com
U.S. Department of Agriculture Meat and Poultry Hot Line	800-535-4555	www.fsis.usda.gov
Weber Grill	800-446-1071	www.weber.com
Wilton Cake Decorating	800-942-8881	www.wilton.com

index

Talk Turkey to Me

W

Z

notes

notes

notes

notes

notes

Talk Turkey to Me

order form

Talk Turkey To Me ($19.95)
is available wherever books are sold, or order online!

Online orders: www.TalkTurkeyToMe.com

Mail orders: Include a copy of this form with your order and mail to:

Wishbone Press and Promotions
PO Box 414
Glen Ellyn, IL 60137

Toll-free telephone orders: Call 1-866-388-8030

Name_____

Address_____

City_____State_____Zip_____

Telephone_____

Email address_____

Sales tax: Illinois residents add 6.75% sales tax. Nevada residents add 7.75% sales tax.

U.S. shipping and handling: $5.95 for the first book and $2.00 for each additional book.

International shipping and handling: Actual shipping rate will be calculated and a 15% handling fee will be added. Estimate $10.00 for the first book and $6.00 for each additional book.

Payment: ❏ Check ❏ Money Order ❏ Visa ❏ MasterCard

Card number_____

Name on card_____Expiration date_____

Renee Ferguson answered America's turkey questions for the Butterball® Turkey Talk-Line™ for more than 14 years. Over those years she fielded thousands of consumer questions during the Thanksgiving and Christmas holiday seasons.

She has collected stories, anecdotes, recipes, and instructions in various cooking and food-preparation techniques and put them into this concise but lighthearted cookbook for anyone who enjoys eating. *Talk Turkey to Me: A Good Time in the Kitchen Talking Turkey and All the Trimmings* is destined to become a colorful addition to the patchwork quilt of American life.

Ferguson is a wife and mother of three who loves to cook. Her gourmet dinner parties have thrilled family and friends over the years. Her simple approach to creative cooking is "if you can read, you can cook." This is the inspiration behind *Talk Turkey to Me: A Good Time in the Kitchen Talking Turkey and All the Trimmings.*